Alan Sroufe is a nationally recognized expert in the field of infant emotional development. He is Professor of Child Psychology, Institute of Child Development, University of Minnesota, and also has an appointment in the Department of Psychiatry, Medical School, University of Minnesota.

Knowing & Enjoying Your Baby

Alan Sroufe

A SPECTRUM BOOK

PRENTICE-HALL, INC., Englewood Cliffs, N.J. 07632

Library of Congress Cataloging in Publication Data

SROUFE, ALAN.
  Knowing and enjoying your baby.

  (A Spectrum Book)
  Includes bibliographies and index.
  1. Infant psychology.   I. Title.
BF723.I6S64   155.4 '22   77-21703
ISBN 0-13-516690-X
ISBN 0-13-516682-9 pbk.

Printed in the United States of America

10 9 8 7 6 5 4 3 2 1

Prentice-Hall International, Inc., *London*
Prentice-Hall of Australia Pty., Limited, *Sydney*
Prentice-Hall of Canada, Ltd., *Toronto*
Prentice-Hall of India Private, Limited, *New Delhi*
Prentice-Hall of Japan, Inc., *Tokyo*
Prentice-Hall of Southeast Asia Pte., Ltd., *Singapore*
Whitehall Books, Limited, *Wellington, New Zealand*

To my daughter, Heather
    Who taught me all she knew
    about laughter and loving and life
And to my mother
    Who teaches us yet.

CONTENTS

Contents

Preface:
A Note to Parents

This book is about the emotional development of your infant. Many books about babies have been written, and a number of them contain useful, accurate information. But in the past these books have emphasized motor, mental, and, to a lesser extent, social development. The emotions and emotional development have been neglected almost totally. Therefore, however accurate, they have been seriously incomplete, because emotional development is what ties together cognitive and social development and behavior. Human infants are emotional beings. They smile, laugh, and cry. They experience joy, anger, and fear and later affection, shame, and defiance. As toddlers they become capable of love, guilt, and pride.

Your relationship can have important positive influences on your infant's emotional growth and health. And it is now completely clear that there is no separation between the emotional and mental aspects of life. The attitude with which your child faces a problem or an opportunity, its confidence in itself, its expectations are as much a part of its cognitive functioning as its inherited I.Q. points. Children vary in intelligence. They also vary in their ability to cope with stress and to enjoy their experience.

I have written this book with one goal in mind— that you will know your baby better and enjoy it more. I can think of no more important result than that your infant- and early child-rearing experience be more positive and more rewarding. If you enjoy your baby, it is my expectation that it will thrive. I wish you well.

INTRODUCTION

Enjoying Your Baby

We were at our wits' end. For three straight weeks, Jessica had been crying or fussing all the time, or so it seemed anyway. After we had come home from the hospital, things had settled down fine, though George seemed to be a little disappointed that she "didn't do very much." But she was healthy and just adorable and I loved her. Then at about five weeks the trouble began. She fussed when I was trying to feed her, when I was changing her, and many times for no apparent reason at all. Her sleep, which had become quite regular, became fitful, and she was crying half the night.

When she was upset like this, nothing seemed to help. Sometimes I thought she must be hungry, but she rejected the breast. I would change her, rock her, or try to soothe her with my voice. George would pace the floor with her, patting—at times I fear, pounding—her on the back. But everything we tried seemed to make the fussing and crying worse. She would be fussing and fussing in her crib, but when we picked her up, she cried all the more. We felt completely frustrated. According to both Dr. Spock and our pediatrician, this was all "perfectly normal," something that happened with *some* babies—just a natural part of growth. They called it "colic," a by-product of a rapidly developing digestive system. "Don't worry, she'll grow out of it," they said, but we were exasperated. Is this what having a baby was going to be?

But she did grow out of it. In part, we thought that we learned better ways to soothe her, but mainly it seemed that she just got feeling better. Her peaceful periods became longer, and she spent more time looking around and playing in her crib. Best yet, she started paying more attention to us. She would follow our movements, listen to our voices, and when we talked to her, she looked right at us and smiled a big, beautiful smile. George would lean over her crib and say, "Come on, you little devil, let's see a big smile for your old Dad, come on, let's see it. Yeah, and we were gonna send you back to the hospital!" We knew that she was ours, and we were hers from then on. It is beautiful. We just love her. I never thought George would be so involved. She really won him over. And me, too.

The development of the human infant is the most fascinating process you ever may encounter. As remarkable as are the dance of a bee, the rhythm of the tides, or the unfolding of a flower, how much more awe-inspiring is the unfolding of the conscious being itself. In less than one year, the infant makes a transition from a primitive, almost purely reflexive organism, primarily asleep or engaged in apparently aimless activity, to a person with the capacity to remember, to react differentially to various aspects of its experience, to produce effects deliberately in its world, and to form a specific attachment relationship with its caregivers. In short, it becomes a conscious being. The year-old is far more like an adult than it is like a newborn.

You are about to witness, participate in, and, I hope, fully enjoy this amazing process. Enjoyment was one of your original motives in having this baby, and during the course of pregnancy, you looked forward to its arrival. To enjoy your baby is a perfectly legitimate and lofty motive. In fact, **4** it is the purpose of this book to expand your

pleasure and fascination in your infant's development through increased observational powers and
an awareness concerning the nature of development. Naturally, you are motivated to care for your infant adequately, but such care is certainly not incompatible with enjoyment; nor should it represent a higher priority concern.

Enjoying Your Baby

This clearly is not a book in which you and I will worry about how your child is going to do in the first grade, though I suspect if you and your baby enjoy each other, first grade will take care of itself. There are several reasons for the stress on enjoying your baby, rather than on "stimulating" your infant's development or enriching the environment. First, as suggested above, this is a learning and experiencing opportunity of a lifetime for you; intellectually and emotionally, your infant's first two years well can be the most richly rewarding experience you have ever known. And *that* is important.

Moreover, we frankly do not know very much about promoting development. Developmental psychology is a very new science, and we are just beginning to learn about the processes of normal psychological growth. We know that under extreme conditions of deprivation, infants do not thrive. But within rather broad limits, the developmental process unfolds with *great* regularity. This, in fact, was the major point of Piaget's famous work.

I say this with complete awareness of and familiarity with the many books written on stimulating infant development. My conclusions are based on research conducted in the 1970s, much of which will be published in late 1977 or 1978. By this date, we know of nothing more important for infant development, including intellectual development, than loving parents and a responsive social environment.

5

On Pots, Pans, Spoons, and Caregiver–Infant Play

The ideas of basic importance in Piaget's work are that infants learn through their actions and that a range of experiences can be adequate for cognitive growth. Infants can turn a spoon over and note its changing appearance, just as they can manipulate a commercial toy. They can bang a spoon on a pan and note the result, just as they can shake a commercial rattle. They can put a yogurt cup inside the oatmeal carton, open and close the cabinet door, and later, look at their changing expressions in the mirror. In all these ways they can coordinate impressions, repeat actions, and produce consequences in the environment, which are the basic stuff of mental growth. Beyond seeing to it that there are safe, manipulable objects around that are of interest to your infant, there is little you need to provide in terms of the physical environment. And if you pay attention, your infant will show you what is of interest at different points in development. *There is at present no data supporting the usefulness of commercial infant stimulation kits or most commercial toys.*[1]

The tendency to thrive is strong in the infant, and basically, promoting development seems simply to be a matter of providing basic conditions. Pots, pans, spoons, and window curtains, as well as the child's own body, are probably as fully adequate tools for learning about the world as are mobiles, puzzles, and "busy boxes" (though each of these

---

[1]Burton White provides some good information on the interests of infants at different ages. As in the present account, he takes a fairly dim view of most commercial products. He does point to the usefulness of the common ball, cradle gyms, mirrors, and manipulable objects. I recommend his book, *The first three years of life,* as a source of ideas on this matter.

can be great fun as well). Interaction and play with you is probably the richest possible format for stimulation of cognitive (mental) abilities. No special apparatus or procedures are required.

Figure 1-1. The most educational objects available to the infant are its own body and those of others. Here a 5-month-old playfully explores a caregiver's face. (Photo: G. & W. Piccolo.)

On the positive side, we do know some very important things about infant development. We know that cognitive (intellectual) and affective-emotional growth are inseparable. As infants develop, cognitive and emotional growth go forward together. Infants learn through play, and learning is expressed in action and in smiling, laughter, crying, and other affects. Similarly, both cognitive and affective development have close ties with social development. It now is becoming clear, for example, that infants learn a great deal that is of fundamental importance within the context of a playful, one-to-one interaction with an adult caregiver. In the context of this play, they learn to pay attention and to focus attention; they learn to "hold" on to themselves as they are being held and **7** to organize responses; they learn to pace and regulate their behavior and to tolerate tension; and they learn a sense of mutual effectance. The world responds *to* them as well as eliciting responses *from* them. These are the very building blocks of all important learning that is to follow. At the same time, the infant's cognitive growth and affective expression contribute to its social relations. (All of these matters are major topics in this book.)

So when you interact with and enjoy your baby, when you tune to its signals and minister to its needs in a sensitive way, and when you engage in the intimate, intricate dance that is caregiver–infant play, you are contributing in a vital way to your infant's development. As you are more in tune with your baby, the baby has more opportunity to draw from your interaction; and the more likely you are to enjoy the infant. The more you enjoy being with your infant, the more likely you are to be in tune with the baby and the baby, being sensitive to your mood, to be positively responsive to you. This is a remarkably simple thesis, but sometimes life is like that. *Your baby needs you to enjoy it.* So learn, be fascinated, enjoy.

Goals for the Book

Like so many things, the nature of the developmental process and specific developmental achievements are easy to see if you know what to look for. A major purpose of this book is to help you get a feel for the biological nature of human psychological development and to alert you to some of the major developmental accomplishments of infancy and to relationships among these. Throughout, there will be an emphasis on the organized nature of development and the meaningfulness of infant behavior. The infant has a sign and signal system that you will learn naturally in the course of events. This book will have served its purpose if you are encouraged to follow your belief that your baby's actions and expressions *do* make sense and if you become more alert to and perceptive of these signals, both to what they do mean and do not mean.

The development of affect expression, especially pleasure and joy, is a central theme in this book. Affective and emotional development has been notably slighted by developmental psychology; yet, the most clear communications of the preverbal infant are affective expressions. Given the integrated nature of human development, cognitive and social growth are reflected by changes in affective responsiveness. Smiling and laughing, for example, are used to illustrate the basic nature of mental processes and especially the nature of mental growth. It is my belief that an understanding of your infant's cognitive development will contribute to your emotional closeness with the infant and to your joy in caregiving. This is true, just as an understanding of your baby's expressions of pleasure, fear, and anger will help you to know about its experience of the world. These matters are discussed in some detail throughout the book. Such a discussion is necessary to make clear the role of your relationship in the overall development of your infant (Chapters 5 and 6). It also can provide the framework for interpretation of your infant's signals and help you to see the growth process as it unfolds.

By attending to changes in the nature of situations producing smiling and laughter in your baby, you will learn a very great deal about infant development. With this example of the meaningfulness of infant behaviors and actions, you will get a basic feel for the nature of infancy. And as you understand the unfolding of the whole range of emotions in relation to other aspects of development, your understanding of the baby will become more complete. If you like, you will be able to check your insights through systematic observation. At the end of the book, specific observation and recording procedures are described. You can keep track systematically of the course of smiling and laughing, the development of stranger fear and separation protest, and other affective developments. At the same time, for example, you can assess the development of memory (object permanence), purposefulness (intentionality), imitation, and certain aspects of motor development in order to verify the integrated, organized nature of development.

In some ways, I have organized this book as the nature of development itself is organized, as a process of combining parts of knowledge into a more comprehensive whole. You will be introduced to pieces of the picture, given different views of these pieces, and continually encouraged to put the pieces together into a more complete framework. Such concepts as the caregiver–infant bond or attachment, for example, will be introduced—then repeatedly worked into later discussions. Your view of the infant and the nature of development will become more and more complete and integrated as you proceed through the book. Also, things that are somewhat vague at first will become clear as you read on. Some of the ideas presented are understood best when looked at from several different perspectives, so they may become meaningful to you only when you are well into the book. The book is constructed in such a way that you can read sections out of sequence without losing the major themes.

A list of the research reports upon which this book is based and other references to interesting, informative papers and books is at the end of each chapter. Brazelton's book, *Infants and mothers,* and Bühler's *The first year of life* were especially important aids in formulating the outline of development provided in Part III. Brazelton's book, which is available in paperback, is an excellent general source on infant development.

In a very real sense, we are learning together. I am sharing with you what I have learned from my own infant and from the sizable number of normal and retarded infants we have studied at the University of Minnesota. And your own learning will be added on top of this. In fact, you are in a position to observe your infant in much more detail than we could observe any of the infants we have studied and even more carefully than I observed my own. It was rather late in her first year before she taught me about the wonders of her development, and I missed a great deal. I have no doubt that you will have insights that have escaped me. If you like, a means has been established at the very end of the book by which you may share what you learn with me and therefore with others. It is my hope that our mutual enjoyment of infants will be enhanced.

Sources

BRAZELTON, T. B. *Infants and mothers.* New York: Delacorte Press, 1969.

BÜHLER, C. *The first year of life.* New York: The John Day Co., 1930.

PIAGET, J. *The origins of intelligence in children.* New York: Routledge & Kegan Paul, 1952.

WHITE, B. *The first three years of life.* Englewood Cliffs, N.J.: Prentice-Hall, Inc., 1975.

2

The Nature of Development

The mental functioning of the ten-month-old is more like that of an adult than like that of a young infant.

The mother of a six-month-old infant puts one end of a cloth in her mouth, then dangles the loose end in front of her baby by shaking her head from side to side. The infant's attention is captured by the .cloth. All activity ceases, and the baby watches the cloth intently. After a period of inspection, the infant methodically reaches for the cloth and pulls it from the mother's mouth, all without a change in the sober expression. Almost inevitably, the cloth shortly finds its way into the baby's own mouth, as does anything the infant grasps at this age.

In the same situation, a ten-month-old first watches with rapt attention, though perhaps glancing back and forth between the cloth and the mother's face. Very quickly the face brightens, and the infant, smiling or laughing, *grabs* the cloth from the mother's mouth. Perhaps signaled by movements of her lips, the infant attempts to stuff

12

the cloth back into the mother's mouth, laughing uproariously (Figure 2-1).

How are these two babies different? What development has taken place during the four months of life separating these two infants? Is there some "thing" that the ten-month-old "has more of" than the six-month-old? Or does it make more sense to think of the ten-month-old as a fundamentally transformed being, qualitatively different from the six-month-old?[1] It seems fairly clear on an observational level that the younger infant becomes engaged with the cloth as a separate entity; that for him or her the mother recedes into the background. The cloth seemingly is pulled from the mother's mouth "inadvertently," as part of the operation of securing the object. No game is discerned; the relationship between cloth and mother is lost. In other words, in the first half-year infants tend to reach for objects that capture their attention, whether a brightly colored ball on the floor, the small, wiggly foot at the end of their leg, or a cloth in mother's mouth. They also tend to stick things they do reach into their mouths.

The ten-month-old, on the other hand, has the ability to keep in mind both the cloth and mother and, more importantly, is able to grasp the relationship between the two (Piaget describes this important ability as the *coordination of schemes*). This infant also must have some kind of memory (image, scheme) for the mother without the cloth, must know that he or she can bring about the reverse transformation (mother without cloth) and can even create the incongruity again. The ten-month-old operates with the aid of a memory,

---

[1]Keep in mind throughout that any ages suggested are meant only as approximations. Development does not occur on a month-by-month basis; it unfolds.

representations of objects (people) or events that can provide a backdrop for current experience. And his/her behavior is influenced by an ability to anticipate outcome. The ten-month-old has a past and a future as well as present experience. It also has a sense of permanence concerning the world, in this case that mother-without-cloth is still there in mother-with-cloth. All of this is reflected in the older infant's laughter in this situation.

There are many ways to describe the developmental difference between these two infants. As is discussed later, the six-month-old is acquiring busily the experience that will let the capacities of the ten-month-old emerge. There is a continuity between the two age periods. But one thing is clear: the ten-month-old is a vastly different and more capable infant than the six-month-old. Tremendous development has taken place during this short time span, and the result is best described in terms of qualitative change rather than quantitative change. The ten-month-old grasped the incongruity; the six-month-old, though perhaps having a vague sense that something unusual was happening, did not grasp it. Similarly, though one can speak of "memory" and "anticipation" in infants during the first half-year, such capacities are qualitatively different than those of the ten-month-old. In fact, in many ways, the mental functioning of the ten-month-old is more like that of an adult than like that of a young infant. And that is the remarkable thing.

Those who have raised a child throughout infancy or who have been in close contact with several infants already understand much of what is being said here. Development is not a gradual, steady process, though it is of course continuous. Rather, it is noticeably uneven, with periods of

Figure 2-1 a, b. The 10-month-old not only understands this game; it attempts to repeat the event as well. (Photo: D. LaSota.)

strikingly rapid psychological and physical growth, all the more remarkable because development in the preceding period already had seemed incredible. One week, after a long period of consolidation, a baby may "just start walking." One week your eight- or ten-week-old may begin smiling at your face with complete regularity, having done it in the past only inconsistently. One week my daughter added verbs to her language and began placing adjectives before nouns ("big cookie" vs. "cookie, big"). You will see many such examples as your baby develops.

Two interrelated concepts are helpful for conceptualizing such periods of rapid development: *converging lines of development* and *developmental reorganization.* Just as it sounds, converging lines of development refer to coordinated changes in various aspects of growth—physical, physiological, cognitive (mental), socioemotional. Reorganization refers to the qualitative change notion just discussed, a fundamental change in the infant's engagement of the world.

The process has been described as increasingly rapid development and consolidation in several **15** spheres to a point where a fundamental transformation of the infant—a new way of operating in the environment—just naturally emerges in response to the force of development.[2] As one example, it is as though sensory impressions of the world were adding up to some critical mass for the emergence of a mental concept. With repeated exposure to the same or similar events, the infant eventually comes to recognize it, and now external events exist in a new way. At the same time, the central nervous system itself is consolidating development in one phase and now is on the threshold of a new phase of development. It is not surprising that research suggests these processes occur in a coordinated, perhaps synchronized manner, because it is reasonable to expect that physiological–neurological development paves the way for cognitive-social-emotional growth and also that sensory-motor-affective experience would contribute to physiological development.

Qualitative Turning Points in Early Development

There are three developmental reorganizations in the first two years of life that command special attention. Interestingly, all are marked by changes in affective (emotional) development, and they are therefore readily observable by you.

The first of these generally occurs between eight and twelve weeks of age. During this time a number of maturational changes occur. Much to your relief, infantile fussiness or colic declines (see the scenario at the beginning of Chapter 1). Your

---

[2]Spitz, Emde, and Metcalf, 1970.

infant who has had periods of fitfulness, which you felt powerless to relieve, begins crying less and sleeping and eating better. The colic was normal (probably indicating rapid development of the digestive system), and so is its diminishing. At the same time, maturational changes in the EEG (brain wave) are apparent, and sleep patterns become more like those of the adult. At first the newborn's sleep was *either* irregular (difficult to distinguish from the awake state) *or* very deep, with rousing being difficult. Periods of REM (rapid eye movement, later associated with dreaming) could occur when awake or asleep, and they often marked the onset of sleep. By ten weeks, however, REM occurs only in sleep, and sleep itself begins without REM and has become differentiated into several forms. These patterns are similar to those of the adult. Also, certain early reflexes (for example, "rooting" and the Babkin, see Chapter 11) disappear. All of these findings point to the maturation of the cortex, that part of the brain associated with higher mental functioning and the voluntary control of behavior.

At the same time, a remarkable social-cognitive development occurs. The newborn sleep smiles disappear during this period, but the social smile becomes prominent. The infant begins smiling with great regularity at any immobile, smiling face in front of him. Since the infant was much more a creature responding to his own visceral (internal) sensations before this time, this switch to responsiveness to the surroundings, marked by smiling to your face and other familiar objects, is a qualitative turn in development making him in many ways more like an adult than a newborn baby. It is from attending to the surroundings that coordinated impressions, reliability of cooccurrences, and permanence of objects will be sensed. Development was rapid before, but now it will explode as the infant has made a fundamental differentiation between the self and the world and is open to its experience in a new way. (More is said about this critical period in Chapters 3 and 7.)

The process repeats itself. From its transactions with the environment, a second critical point is reached between about six and ten months. Repeated experience with objects in multiple ways leads the infant to put these impressions together into a concept of the object. From being the touchable, seeable, hearable, smellable collection of experiences, mother becomes *she who* touches, talks to, smiles at, and holds—she becomes mother, a specific object with an existence that continues even when I cannot see her.[3] Generally, a critical mass of experiences with the surroundings in the present leads the infant to form internalized images that keep the objects in experience even when they are not present and enables the baby to anticipate outcomes before they occur.

In short, the ability to recognize objects during the first period (as in the smile to the face) ultimately leads to the ability to recall objects even when they are not present. With these capacities of memory and anticipation, the infant becomes sensitive to sequence of events and context. Its behavior becomes much more complexly motivated—by what has just happened, by what has happened in this situation before, and by what is about to happen, rather than merely by immediate circumstance. Without doubt, advances in nervous system development parallel these psychological changes.

---

[3] I am indebted to my former student, Everett Waters, for this formulation.

And in the affective (emotional) sphere, the development of genuine fear and anger occurs, and the capacity for joy expands. Fear, for example, as opposed to startle or distress, involves a categorical judgment on the part of the infant: "This is *one of those* and I don't like it!" Such a reaction requires memory. The most familiar fear to develop is so-called stranger anxiety. In our studies we have confirmed the onset of fearful reactions to unfamiliar persons between about seven and ten months, though the reaction may be quite subtle. To show fear of strangers, infants must distinguish among people. Fear, in general, requires memory and considerable organization and differentiation of experience. As will be discussed in Chapter 5, the expression of fear is also quite sensitive to situational circumstances (context). There are also interesting developments in smiling and laughter during this period. In fact, a close developmental and psychological relationship between laughter and fear will become apparent (see Chapter 5).

As a purposeful being in a world of permanent objects that can be acted on in a planned way, the infant moves toward a third developmental reorganization. Many developmental theorists have described the emergence of autonomy in the second year, the emergence of the infant as a separate being with self-awareness. Some emphasize exploration, some emphasize the discovery of will, and some emphasize the growth of symbolic representation and language. In any case, the increased capacity for internal representation, object mastery skills, and mobility *converge* to support the infant's use of the caregiver as a base for exploration. This experience in mastering the environment on one's own (moving out from the caregiver) necessarily leads to the emergence of the autonomous self and to qualitative changes in the child's transactions with the environment. The child who can hold multiple elements in mind at the same time can manipulate the environment in novel ways (e.g., go get the horse from the barn and put it in front of the wagon). The child who has beginning language can cope with its emotions in a new way. For example, when you leave it may talk about your absence as it waits for your return. And the child who is becoming aware of its independence can refuse to comply with your requests. This turning point is marked by the onset of shame, defiance, genuine affection, and positive self-evaluation, which is the root of pride. Much more will be said about these matters in Chapters 9 and 10.

Development as Organized and Tied Together

A fundamental quality of development, apparent in the three stages just described, concerns its integrated nature. Various aspects of development do not occur separately; each sphere of psychological growth is influenced by each other sphere, and they go forward in an interlocking manner. Cognitive (mental) development influences social–emotional development, and social–emotional development influences cognitive development. Thus, the reliable social smile reveals the infant's recognition of the face. Similarly, in the second half of the first year of life, when you see the infant in your care express genuine fear and anger (as opposed to the diffuse distress or rage reactions of earlier months), you will know several things. You will know that he or she has goal directedness (intentionality), a functioning memory, and some sense of persons as entities separate from him- or herself. You will know the angry infant has intentions, for example, because anger will be expressed only as the infant is capable of pursuing and sustaining action toward a goal and finds its actions blocked. On the other hand, when your infant's smiles of recognition and pleasure foster your enjoyment in interaction, the infant's cognitive development will be enhanced. The infant's developing social behavior alters the way you are with the infant, and this ultimately contributes to its cognitive growth. And so it goes with the cognitive realm now leading, the social now leading, but development going forward as an integrated process.

A final quality of development is its hierarchically organized nature. You will run into this notion a lot in reading about physical and motor development, but it applies to psychological development as well. The idea is quite simple and has close ties to biology. In terms of motor development, hierarchical organization means that various subacts are put together into (made subordinate parts of) a complex act. Infants first learn the skills underlying crawling or walking and then put them together into the total act. Similarly with psychological development, cognitive achievements are not discarded; they are organized into a more complex framework. To be sure, this transforms the meaning and function of the cognitive achievement, as is also the case when acts are organized and tied together into more complex acts. The whole is more than the sum of the parts. This is true throughout biology. The eye is a part of the visual system within a complex organism. Without the rest of the system, it would not be very interesting; it certainly would not be an eye. Its meaning is derived from its relationship to the hierarchically organized structure of which it is a part.

So this is the process of development—not even, not gradual, but erupting, unfolding, organic. It is a process that to look for is to see. It is the very nature of your baby. Three critical periods of development have been called to your attention. You perhaps will discern others. You certainly will get a feel for the complexity of the reorganizations described above and for the way in which the first leads to the second, the second to the third. Try especially to note concurrent developments. Note, for example, the relationship between motor achievements (holding the head up, directed reaching, scooting and crawling), affective expression, vocal behavior, exploration, and memory development. Note also how the growth of purposefulness (intent) and stages in imitation—from contagion to literal, to nonliteral, to deferred—are related to the major reorganizations of development (see Chapter 8). And especially, pay close attention to your infant's smiling, laughing, and play. Try to note relationships between smiling and the development of visual attention (following), motor development, and signs of cognitive growth. When does smiling to your face occur with great regularity? When does the baby smile to *your* face but become sober when the face is that of an unfamiliar person? When does he or she laugh in anticipation of your return in peekaboo? Or first laugh repeatedly at an action he or she does?

In the next two chapters I describe the developmental course of smiling and laughter. The types of situations that produce these reactions at different points in development are pointed out to illustrate the integrated nature of development. Your infant will be seen as an active participant in its own development. The infant's inborn motivation to develop will become clear as will the naturalness of the process. As we proceed, an increasingly integrated picture of development is presented, with an outline of development in the first year provided in Chapter 7. An integration of the various aspects of development, with special attention to the unfolding of the emotions, is presented in Chapter 8. Chapters 9 and 10 summarize the whole process, as well as carry it into the second year.

Sources

BREGER, L. *From instinct to identity: The development of personality*. Englewood Cliffs, N.J.: Prentice-Hall, Inc., 1974.

EMDE, R. GAENSBAUER, T., & HARMON, R. Emotional expression in infancy: A biobehavioral study. *Psychological Issues Monograph Series,* 1976.

PIAGET, J. *The origins of intelligence in children.* New York: Routledge & Kegan Paul, 1952.

SPITZ, R., EMDE, R., & METCALF, E. Further prototypes of ego formation. *Psychoanalytic Study of the Child,* 1970, *25,* 417–44.

SROUFE, L. A. Wariness of strangers and the study of infant development. *Child Development,* Sept. 1977.

SROUFE, L. A., WATERS, E., & MATAS, L. Contextual determinants of infant affective response. In M. Lewis & L. Rosenblum (Eds.), *The origins of fear.* New York: John Wiley, 1974.

AFFECT & PLAY:
THE PROCESS
OF DEVELOPMENT

Smiling: The Infant Engages Its World

3

Although it has an important social function, the smile also appears to be an open window through which we may view one aspect of cognitive functioning in infants.

ZELAZO & KOMER, from *Child Development,* 1971

In the very beginning the newborn most frequently smiles while it is *asleep* (Figure 3-1). These tiny smiles, involving only a turning up of the corners of the mouth, are called "spontaneous," because they occur in the absence of sounds, lighting changes, or other external events. They apparently are triggered by some event or process *inside* the infant. Spontaneous (or endogenous) smiles are not caused by "gas," as is sometimes thought, nor by a hunger state. You may, of course, sometimes see such smiles at the same time as you observe gastric activity, but gas certainly is not the primary cause for the smiles. For one thing, these smiles occur primarily (often only) during sleep, and gastric activity is not restricted to sleep periods. Also, studies have shown specifically that spontaneous smiles are not related to time-since-feeding or to gastric activity.

The most compelling theory is that spontaneous smiles are related to fluctuating states of excitation in the baby's nervous system. Babies are sometimes more fully relaxed and sometimes more aroused. During sleep such fluctuations also seem to occur, even though the excitation level generally would be rather low. The spontaneous smile, then, reflects relaxation below some threshold, a downward fluctuation in the infant's resting excitation or arousal state. The excitation level increases slightly, then falls back down with the smile muscles relaxing as part of this (see Figure 3-2). One bit of evidence concerning this model is that spontaneous smiles tend to occur in bursts during REM (rapid eye movement) sleep. This type of "irregular" sleep is characterized by low and probably fluctuating levels of arousal. You might imagine that the state of excitation of the nervous system is hovering right near our critical threshold during REM sleep, and this is why a number of these tiny smiles can occur in a short time. If the infant is startled, however, this would raise the level of excitation, and no further smiles could occur until the level of arousal slowly dropped down below the threshold again (see Figure 3-2). This is exactly what observers have reported.[1] Robert Emde, a prominent researcher at the University of Colorado Medical School, also has reported that in rousing infants from sleep toward wakefulness, bursts of tiny smiles occur, just as one would expect from the model.

These spontaneous smiles should not be thought of as indicating pleasure (or even conscious experience in that sense), though they might be thought of as reflecting a pleasant state. They are

---

[1]Wolff, P. Observations on the early development of smiling. In B. M. Foss (Ed.), *Determinants of infant behaviour II*. London: Methuen, 1963.

associated with lower brain activity. We know this because they are more common in premature infants and occur in infants lacking a cortex (the more advanced part of the brain). They cease occurring as the infant matures beyond the first eight to twelve weeks of life. They are related to later smiles not because they embody their meaning (that is, expressions of pleasure) but because, as we shall see, the later, elicited smiles involve the basic, excitation–relaxation process of the spontaneous smiles.

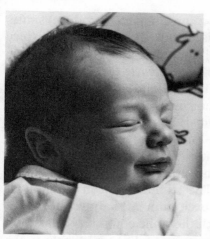

Figure 3-1. The spontaneous sleep smile. (Photo: T. Hopmann.)

Figure 3-2. Schematic illustration of the excitation-relaxation cycle, showing hypothetical threshold and relationship to overt behaviors.

You may be able to observe these spontaneous smiles. When your infant is sleeping lightly, with shallow breathing and without stirring, you will notice a flickering movement of the closed eyelids (*R*apid *E*ye *M*ovements). Often you will notice this as the infant becomes drowsy following feeding. In the midst of such a period you will see a series of these funny little smiles, which while frequent are often ephemeral. The lips often twist and curl up on the ends, giving the appearance of a "Peanuts" character from the Schulz cartoon series (Figure 3-1).

Quite early you can also *elicit* (produce) smiles when your baby is asleep. A high-pitched voice (baby talk), a rhythmic rattling or chime, blowing on the stomach, or other *gentle* tactile stimulation may be the most effective. The smiles are again tiny and occur only after a delay (usually between about six and eight seconds). In many ways these smiles are similar to the spontaneous smiles of sleep, except that the excitation fluctuation was produced by an external event rather than just being a spontaneous process. The stimulation can be thought of as boosting the excitation level above the "critical threshold," with the smile coming as relaxation follows and the arousal falls again below the threshold (see model in Figure 3-2). This situation is something like what happens when the sleeping infant is startled, except that here the gentle stimulation does not raise the arousal level quite so high. The smile can follow more quickly.

There are wide individual variations, but soon—in the first weeks of life—you will be able to elicit smiles when the baby is awake. Some babies give alert smiles in the very first week, others not until the third or fourth week. Babies, of course, differ in maturity and gestational age at birth, and maturation is the basic determinant of development in the early weeks. Two weeks difference in age during the newborn period is striking, though later on in the first year it will not be so noticeable. There is absolutely no evidence at this point that age of first alert smiles, within very broad limits, is related to later development or intelligence. It is important that you know about the great individual variation in infant development, that any ages stated in this book are meant only to be rough approximations. Should your infant exhibit a behavior earlier or later than suggested here, you should not reach conclusions concerning intellectual level. Focus on sequence of events, the process. This is the fascinating part. If you do, I have no doubt you will conclude your infant is remarkable. The intricacies of development are always amazing.

Regardless of the exact ages, there does seem to be a series of steps or stages that most infants go through in developing awake smiles. First, it seems to be easiest to elicit smiles while the infant is drowsy, perhaps following a feeding. Later, it is possible to get a smile when the infant is alert and following some event with its eyes, for example, the movement of your head. Still, the most effective stimulation in the first two or three weeks is of a gentle, repetitive, modulated nature; at least, that is the conclusion from the evidence we now have. Finally, usually by about the fourth week, more intense stimulation can be used (for example, three vigorous bounces of the hands—a form of pat-a-cake). *The smiles to such intense events are correspondingly big, open-mouth smiles* (Figure 3-3), probably involving some movement of the head and vocalization (gurgling sounds, rather than the laugh you will hear at age three or four months). **31**

Smiling In Table 3-1 it can be seen that while the situations that produce smiles are changing over the first three to six weeks, the smile itself also is getting bigger with increasing involvement of the eyes and mouth and that it occurs more quickly following stimulation (has a shorter latency). This is a sequence you probably can see unfold.

Table 3–1: The Development of Smiling and Laughter

Age	Response	Stimulation	Latency	Remarks
SMILING				
Neonate	Corners of the mouth	No external stimulation		Due to CNS fluctuations
Week 1	Corners of the mouth	Low level, modulated	6-8 sec.	During sleep, boosting of tension
Week 2	Mouth pulled back	Low level, modulated; voices		When drowsy, satiated
Week 3	Grin, including eyes	Moderate level, voices	4-5 sec.	When alert, attentive (nodding head with voice)
Week 4	Grin, active smile	Moderate, or moderately intense	Reduced	Vigorous tactile stimulation effective
Weeks 5-8	Grin, active smile, cooing	Dynamic stimulation, first visual stimulation	3 sec. or less	Nodding head, flicking lights, stimulation that must be followed
Weeks 8-12	Grin, active smile, cooing	Static, visual stimulation, moderately intense	Short	Trial-by-trial effects, effortful assimilation, recognition; static at times more effective than dynamic
LAUGHTER				
Month 4	Laughter	Multimodal, vigorous stimulation	1-2 sec.	Tactile, auditory
Months 5-6	Laughter	Intense auditory stimulation, as well as tactile	Immediate	Items that previously may have caused crying
Months 7-9	Laughter	Social, visual stimulation, primarily dynamic	Immediate	Tactile, auditory decline
Months 10-12	Laughter	Visual, social	Immediate or in anticipation	Visual incongruities, active participation

As the infant progresses through this sequence of limited smiles to gentle stimulation while drowsy to full-faced, active smiles while alert, it is clear that it is becoming capable of handling or dealing with more tension. It is as though the infant can convert the intensity of the stimulation into the vigor of the smile. The increasing capacity of the system to tolerate faster, sharper tension swings probably implies the very beginnings of cortical (higher brain) development. The infant apparently can impose patterning on the stimulation and thus

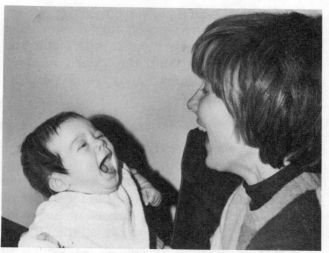

Figure 3-3. Broad, active smile of a 7-week-old to dynamic face-to-face stimulation by caregiver. (Photo: H. Wray.)

modify its impact. Instead of being distressing, it is pleasurable. Earlier, vigorous stimulation well may lead to distress.

One important feature of development that you will see again and again is the infant's tendency to continually move toward more active participation in its own experience. For example, while

33

visual stimulation is not very effective in producing smiles at first, Peter Wolff found that by the fourth week, a nodding head with high-pitched voice was more likely to elicit smiling than a voice alone. And in the following weeks, dynamic visual stimulation (blinking lights, rotating mobile, nodding head without voice, and so on) became quite effective. Since, unlike intrusive tactile and auditory stimulation, visual stimulation requires directed attention by the infant, the tension here is more a product of interaction between the infant and the stimulation. In contrast to the next period, however, stimulus *content* probably still is not very important; rather, the crucial features are probably rhythm, repetition, and modulation, as was the case with tactile and auditory stimulation. Still, this period marks a transition for the infant away from passively receiving stimulation.

The Meaning of the "Social" Smile

By age three months, and often by age eight to ten weeks, a remarkable development in the course of smiling occurs. The infant begins smiling with *regularity* at static (nonmoving) visual stimuli. The most striking situation, of course, is the smile to the human face. When fullface in front of the infant, as opposed to exhibiting a profile, you and others can elicit smiles from your infant over and over. Though the infant will smile at mobiles (Figure 3-4), dolls, and other objects with which it is familiar, the response to the face is so reliable that early elicited smiles once were referred to as social smiles.

And what is so remarkable about this? If you grant that the tension fluctuation notion explains why the smile occurs (more evidence for this idea will be presented here and in the next two chapters), then you must ask what causes the tension-relaxation process in this case. It is easy to see how noises and tactile (touching) stimulation might produce increases in excitation that would be followed by relaxation and smiling, and even how this also could occur with dynamic visual stimulation if the infant was attentive. But how is it that the face, which attracted the infant's attention earlier, only now regularly produces the tension–relaxation necessary for the smile? Clearly, *the tension here must be more a function of cognitive (mental) processes* on the part of the infant; that is, the content of the event, rather than physical stimulation per se. The most widely held belief is that with experience the infant has begun to form a model of the face in his or her developing cortex. When it now sees a face, it exerts effort to compare or match this experience with the somewhat vague internal model. It is the *cognitive effort* that is the source of the tension, and it is the success in this rough matching (assimilation) process that leads to relaxation. There is tension, relaxation, and the smile.

That this interpretation is a sensible one is made clear by the decline of smiling to immobile, static faces that occurs after three or four months, even though smiling to your animated, continually changing face continues. Jerome Kagan[2] has written about the decline of smiling to the face in the following way:

> The smile declines because his schema for a face becomes so well articulated that all faces or representations of faces are immediately recognized as such. There is no tension; no effort is required for assimilation, and hence, no smile (Kagan, 1971).

---

[2]J. Kagan, *Change and continuity in infancy.*

Smiling to static visual events is not restricted to the face. On the contrary, by age three months infants will smile at a great many visual stimuli if they are given enough exposure. In a typical study that you could repeat yourself with your baby, Shultz and Zigler found that at first the infants merely looked at a clown they were shown. After a number of presentations, however, the infants began *smiling* at the clown. They did so sooner and more frequently with a stationary clown than with a moving clown (in contrast to the earlier tendency to smile at moving or changing stimulation). Most interesting, with continued presentations of the clown, the infants *stopped* smiling.

The interpretation of this study and a number of others with similar results is clear. At first, having little or no experience with this object, no model of the clown has been internalized. Therefore, try though he or she may, the model- (or scheme-) matching process cannot occur. Tension may be produced by the cognitive effort, but the relaxation does not follow. With repeated presentations, however, the infant does construct such a model and finally, with great effort, is able to match the presented clown to the internalized scheme; that is, *she or he recognizes it!* Ultimately, the infant stops smiling not because the clown is no longer recognized but because it is recognized without much effort. Both effort (tension) and recognition are necessary to produce the tension-relaxation cycle required for the smile.

The world's foremost observer of children, Swiss psychologist–epistemologist Jean Piaget, is responsible for many of the central concepts here, so it would be well to restate his position in his **36** terms. He referred to these smiles as reflecting "recognitory assimilation." At first, being unable to *assimilate* (incorporate) the visual stimulus into any existing framework, the infant *accommodates,* that is, begins altering existing mental structures to include this new object among things known. During this accommodation phase there can be no smile, because effort is great and there is no sense of completion. With the changed structures, the clown now can be assimilated. It fits. There is completion, relaxation, and the smile.

Figure 3-4. Following inspection, excitement and smiling in a 4-month-old to two brightly colored birds. (Photo: G. & W. Piccolo.)

In light of this view, we may say that the three-month-old infant smiles at any face, because faces are recognized rather quickly as such (visually mastered), though with some effort. The stationary clown is more effective than the moving clown, because it is more readily mastered. Older infants smile sooner to presentations of a novel object, because they can master it more quickly.

37

Smiling as a Window
to the Infant's World

Reviewing these points you also may see a connection between the reliable, social smile and awareness, that is, awareness of events in the surroundings. The smile is to a particular event—for example, the clown. If after three or four trials you substitute a stuffed animal for the clown, you will prevent the smile or stop it if it was occurring. The infant again will be soberly attentive as it seeks to accommodate to this new event. It is because the smile is produced by *particular* events and thus represents a connection between the infant and the object (a subjective relationship), that we can say there is awareness and also the genuine emotion of *pleasure.*

The relationship between smiling and mastery continues as the infant develops, and an increasingly active role for the infant is apparent. Piaget speaks of "pleasure at being a cause" being added to recognitory pleasure at about age five months. Infants master their world through action; they smile and, as we shall see in the next chapter, laugh at things they do. Smiling also seems to be associated with problem solving, a later form of mastery. Jerome Kagan of Harvard University reports that two-year-old toddlers smile upon finding a figure hidden in a complex picture. The more difficult the problem, the more likely the smile upon solution!

If you have followed and largely accepted the ideas just presented, you will understand why a number of psychologists see the smile as so closely linked to cognitive (mental) processes. If young infants smile upon effortful assimilation, then we have clues as to what lies at the edge of their developing concepts. If the repetition effects described above reflect model-building, then we can learn something about that process by observing smiling. (For example, by the end of the first year smiling to static visual stimuli becomes infrequent, probably because infants at this age can construct models of simple visual displays with great ease.) In short, observation of smiling (and laughter) helps us to understand what the infant knows and how its developing mind functions.

Consider the developmental change in smiling to faces. At first, the infant smiles at most faces with about equal frequency. He has a visual concept for *face* (awareness of faces) but not for a particularized concept. Soon, however, perhaps by the fourth month, he will smile more frequently at the sight of the caregiver's face than the sight of an unfamiliar face. In a sense, he now recognizes *you*. As this process becomes more complete, perhaps by six months, he will smile at your face, especially if you are smiling and animated; but he may not smile at all at an unfamiliar person at close range. He may be quite sober or even become distressed with extended visual contact with a stranger. His view of persons has become more differentiated, more well developed.

Differentiation is reflected more generally in smiling. At about age five months infants will smile at a variety of simple things. You will see your infant lying on the floor, kicking its feet, and smiling and cooing at the ceiling or a flickering shadow on the wall. Or you can lean over from the couch, talk baby talk, and bob your head around and elicit smiles time after time. But a few months later the smile will be much more selective. There is increasing precision in the smile as the world of the infant becomes more organized.

You may be wondering about explanations of the smile other than the tension–release notion, with **39** its implications for cognitive development. Isn't the smile a reflection of pleasure? What about its obvious communication value?

Certainly the smile is an expression of pleasure, at least following the neonatal period. The point is this: Not only does your infant experience pleasure in greeting you or in the surprising reappearance of Jack from the box. He/she also experiences pleasure in recognizing a heretofore unknown visual display or in repeating an action just discovered. There is pleasure and joy in mastery.

And certainly the smile is a prominent signal to caregivers. It expresses well-being. It elicits approach from you and encourages variations as well as repetitions of your actions (who can ignore the infant's smile!). It provides the opportunity for the beginnings of reciprocity. You can smile at your infant, and your infant can smile at you. You can elicit smiles from your infant, and your infant can elicit smiles from you. Each of you learns that you can affect the other. In part through eye-to-eye contact and smiling, you experience the beginnings of truly mutual interaction; you are joined together.

But none of these social functions of the smile is in competition with the tension–release function. These functions are complementary. As Kagan has stated, "The smile serves many masters"; and this is especially true as the infant and toddler develop. As you know, smiles become stylistic and at times even purposeful. Different children smile in different circumstances. Children smile when they are embarrassed, when they do not understand something, and in anticipation of some pleasure. I do not mean to oversimplify; it is an increasingly complex business. Still, the tension production–tension release process is basic, and I continue to develop this idea in subsequent chapters.

EMDE, R., GAENSBAUER, T., & HARMON, R. Emotional expression in infancy: A biobehavioral study. *Psychological Issues Monograph Series,* 1976.

KAGAN, J. *Change and continuity in infancy.* New York: John Wiley and Sons, Inc., 1971.

PIAGET, J. *The origins of intelligence in children.* New York: Routledge & Kegan Paul, 1952.

SHULTZ, T., & ZIGLER, E. Emotional concomitants of visual mastery in infants: The effects of stimulus movement on smiling and vocalizing. *Journal of Experimental Child Psychology,* 1970, *10,* 390–402.

SROUFE, L. A., & WATERS, E. The ontogenesis of smiling and laughter. A perspective on the organization of development in infancy. *Psychological Review,* 1976, *83,* 173–89.

WOLFF, P. Observations on the early development of smiling. In B. Foss (Ed.), *Determinants of infant behaviour. II.* London: Methuen, 1963.

ZELAZO, P., & KOMER, M. Infant smiling to nonsocial stimuli and the recognition hypothesis. *Child Development,* 1971, *42,* 1937–39.

4

Infant Laughter & the Relationship between Emotional & Cognitive Growth

The proof that the little prince existed was that he was charming, that he laughed, and that he was looking for a sheep.

ANTOINE DE SAINT-EXUPERY, *The Little Prince*

As the first smiles to your face filled you with warmth, the infant's laughter cannot fail to make you happy. You will find yourself eager to repeat successful events and to discover new ones. In addition, laughter, like the smile, reflects important cognitive developments.

Most infants begin to laugh by about age three or four months. Parents often refer to the earlier gurgling smiles as laughter, but the laugh that usually appears now is an unmistakable chortle. It sounds very much like the laugh of the mature child or adult. Laughter occurs immediately or just a second or two following stimulation. It is the maximum smiling response, being qualitatively more intense than other smiles. It reflects a very sharp tension swing, a rapid increase in excitation followed quickly by relaxation.[1]

Not surprisingly, situations effective in eliciting the earliest laughter tend to be very intrusive, as was the case with much smiling in the first two months. For laughter, the stimulation also must be very vigorous (Figure 4-1). In a sizable number of four-month-olds we have observed in a standard mother–infant play situation, only such stimulation as kissing the infant vigorously on the stomach and playing "I'm Gonna Getchu" consistently produced laughter with any babies at this age. In "I'm Gonna Getchu" the mother stands about four feet away from the infant who is in an infant seat. As she says, "I' . . . m Gon . . . na . . ." (with these two words very protracted), she is stepping

Figure 4-1. Four-month-old laughing at being bounced on caregiver's knee. (Photo: G. & W. Piccolo.)

---

[1]Daniel Berlyne has referred to this as an "arousal jag."

and leaning toward her infant with both arms pointed toward the baby and index fingers wiggling. Just as she says "Getchu," in a very chopped-off fashion, she projects her head toward the baby's stomach and pokes the sides of the ribs with both fingers. This is a very stimulating, exciting situation. So is kissing the infant's stomach. And so is bouncing the baby vigorously, which also can produce laughter at a young age.

Figure 4-2. Six-month-old laughing in response to vigorous stimulation (kissing stomach). (Photo: Hunt Greene.)

The point is that, generally, a great deal of tension is required for laughter, and stimulation must be vigorous and intense to produce laughter in the beginning. In fact, the type of stimulation required is so vigorous that it sometimes produces *crying,* especially before the age of laughter. When it occurs, crying probably indicates that the infant's system is not yet capable of such sharp tension swings, since it frequently happens that one month later the baby will laugh at the very items that previously made it cry. The situations still are producing great excitation, but now the infant has the capacity to modulate (modify) this arousal, to transform (assimilate) some portion of the stimulation, promoting a fast recovery following the tension increase. It laughs rather than cries. This is a very important observation about early development, and we will return to this point in Chapter 5.

In the months that follow its appearance, there are important changes in the situations that cause laughter. There is a remarkable continuation and repetition of the process observed with smiling in the first three months. In a manner strikingly parallel to elicited smiles, our research has shown a progression in situations producing laughter from intrusive, vigorous stimulation to subtle visual stimulation, in which the content of the event is of greatest importance (see Table 4-1 as well as Table 3-1 in Chapter 3).

The results presented in Table 4-1, which will be described in words below, are based on a longitudinal study of a small sample (10) of male infants. The procedures for administering the items are found in Table 4-2. These babies were seen each month between the ages of four and twelve months, and the observations were made very carefully. The infant's mother presented each item up to six times, unless the infant laughed on two consecutive presentations or in the very rare event that crying occurred. (The items were presented in a different order for each baby each month.) The results from this study are consistent with those of two studies comparing infants at different ages and are supported in an important way by a study of retarded infants.

These results can be summarized in several different ways, all of which indicate the progression from stimulation-produced laughter to "interpretive" laughter or anticipatory laughter. Table 4-1 simply shows the percentage of infants laughing at least once to each item at each age.

Table 4–1: Percentage of Laughter by Activity for the Longitudinal Study

				Age of Babies in Months				
Activities	4	5	6	7	8	9	10	11	12

AUDITORY

Activities	4	5	6	7	8	9	10	11	12
1. Lip-popping	0	10	0	0	0	0	10	0	10
2. Aaah	0	20	33	33	13	0	40	55	40
3. Boom, boom	0	40	11	22	25	0	20	0	20
4. Synthesizer	0	20	0	0	0	0	0	0	10
5. Whispering	0	0	11	0	0	0	0	0	10
6. Squeaky voice	0	0	0	0	25	0	0	11	40
7. Horse sound	0	0	0	44	0	0	20	22	10

TACTILE

Activities	4	5	6	7	8	9	10	11	12
8. Blowing in hair	0	0	0	11	0	0	10	11	20
9. Kissing stomach	33	30	44	77	50	43	20	33	50
10. Coochy-coo	0	20	22	44	25	14	30	0	0
11. Bouncing on knee	0	20	11	22	25	29	20	22	30
12. Jiggling baby	0	30	33	44	13	29	30	0	40
13. Tickling under chin	0	10	33	11	25	29	10	22	0
14. Mouthing back of neck	0	0	11	11	25	14	20	0	20

SOCIAL

Activities	4	5	6	7	8	9	10	11	12
15. Walking fingers (last trial)	17	20	11	33	25	29	20	22	30
16. Playing tug	0	20	22	33	25	43	20	11	20
17. Cloth in mouth	0	10	11	33	50	14	30	44	50
17. Gonna getchu (last trial)	50	30	44	77	63	43	30	33	70
19. Covering baby's face	0	0	22	22	38	29	20	22	40
20. Stick out tongue	0	0	11	22	13	0	40	33	60
21. Peekaboo	0	10	11	55	38	0	10	11	30

VISUAL

Activities	4	5	6	7	8	9	10	11	12
22. Covered face	0	10	33	55	38	14	30	11	50
23. Disappearing object	0	10	11	11	25	0	30	0	30
24. Sucking baby bottle	0	0	0	11	13	0	40	11	40
25. Crawling on floor	0	10	11	11	50	29	30	22	60
26. Walking like a penguin	0	0	22	22	25	14	10	0	40
27. Shaking hair	0	0	11	44	38	57	40	66	50
28. Human mask	17	0	11	33	13	29	80	33	40

EXTRA

Activities	4	5	6	7	8	9	10	11	12
29. Chasing	0	0	22	22	13	14	50	55	80
30. Holding in air	0	10	22	33	13	43	50	22	40
31. Mirror	0	10	22	33	0	0	0	0	0
32. Gonna getchu (all trials)	50	40	55	77	75	57	50	33	90
33. Walking fingers (all trials)	0	20	11	44	38	43	60	22	80
Number of Babies Tested	*(6)*	*(10)*	*(9)*	*(9)*	*(8)*	*(7)*	*(10)*	*(9)*	*(10)*

Table 4–2: Instructions for Individual Items*

AUDITORY

1. Four pops in a row, then pause. Starts with lips pursed, cheeks full.
2. Starts low, then crescendo in a loud voice, abrupt cutoff. Six-second pause.
3. Using a loud, deep voice pronounce, "Boom, boom, boom," at one-second intervals.
4. Mechanical type of sound, varying voice pitch from low to high and back down again. (Say "pu pu pu pa pa pa pu pu.")
5. With mouth one foot from baby's ear, whisper, "Hi, baby, how are you?" Avoid blowing in ear.
6. Falsetto voice (like Mickey Mouse), say, "Hi, baby, how are you?"
7. With lips relaxed, blow through them as a horse does when he is tired.

TACTILE

8. Blow gently at hair for three seconds. Blow from the side, across the top of his head.
9. Four quick pecks on bare stomach.
10. Gently stroke cheek three times with soft object.
11. Place baby on knees facing away. Five vigorous bounces.
12. Hold baby waist high, horizontal, face toward floor, and jiggle vigorously for three seconds.
13. Using finger, gently tickle under baby's chin for three seconds.
14. Open mouth wide, press lips on back of neck, and create a suction for two seconds.

SOCIAL

15. Focus baby's attention on your fingers. Walk fingers toward baby, then give baby a poke in the ribs. If laughter is achieved, do another trial *not* followed by poking.
16. Allow baby to grasp yarn, then tug three times, trying not to pull it away from him. Pause to repeat.
17. Put cloth in mouth and lean close enough for baby to grasp. Allow baby to pull cloth out and replace it if this is his tendency. Place the end of the cloth in his hand if this is necessary.
18. Say lyrically, "I'm gonna getchu" ("I'm" quite protracted) while leaning toward baby with hands poised to grab. Then grab baby around stomach. If laughter is achieved, do another trial *not* followed by grabbing.
19. Stand at baby's side. If he does not uncover his face immediately, uncover for him. Do not drag cloth across baby's face. Emphasis is on baby getting out from underneath.
20. Stick out tongue until baby touches it (make his hand touch it if necessary). Quickly pull tongue back in as soon as he touches it.
21. Using blank cardboard, get baby's attention with face uncovered, cover face for two seconds, uncover quickly, and pause three seconds. Do *not* say "Peekaboo."

*Pauses between trials are four seconds unless otherwise stated. Numbers correspond to items in Table 4-1.

VISUAL

22. Using a white cloth, proceed as in #28 below.
23. Use one of baby's favorite toys. Focus his attention on it (out of reach). Cover it two seconds, uncover quickly.
24. First make sure that the baby is not hungry, then take bottle, bring toward lips, take three pretend sucks, lower bottle.
25. Place baby in high chair or infant seat. Crawl *across* his field of vision, *not* toward him. *Stand,* return to starting point.
26. Stand with arms to sides, hands extended, walk in an exaggerated waddle, across baby's field of vision. Return to starting point walking normally.
27. Shake head vigorously at a distance of one foot from baby's face three times. Do not allow hair to touch baby.
28. Obtain baby's attention. Hold mask up so he can see it. Place mask in front of your face, lean slowly to within one foot of baby's face, pause two seconds. Lean back slowly, remove mask slowly.

EXTRA ITEMS

29. Crawl behind baby, ostentatiously chasing, slapping hands on floor.
30. Lift baby slowly to position overhead, looking down back. Minimize tactile and kinesthetic aspects.
31. To reduce peekaboo effects, move baby slowly in front of full-length mirror. Hold three seconds, remove slowly, then pause four seconds.
32. As in #18.
33. As in #15.

Toward Active Participation: A Summary of Table 4-1

As stated above, of the twenty-eight basic items in our battery, one-third of the four-month-olds laughed only at "kissing stomach" and "I'm gonna getchu." Five-month-olds laughed at both of these items, and at a resounding "Boom boom boom." This is an intense auditory item and may well have produced distress if the infant were not watching the mother at the time, if someone other than the mother was the agent (especially with somewhat older babies), or if the infant was only two or three months old. Occasionally, it produced crying in four-month-olds. But it was an excellent stimulus for laughter in our five-month-olds.

With these particular infants, the beginnings of a transition could be seen in two ways at six months. One-third or more still laughed at "kissing stomach" and "Gonna Getchu," and they also laughed at the "swelling Aah with abrupt cutoff," another intense auditory item. But they also laughed at being gently jiggled and tickled under the chin, suggesting a greater involvement of certain cognitive processes (perhaps associations with vigorous jiggling or tickling or discerning the rhythmic features of the stimulation). And they laughed at the mother approaching with cloth-covered face. At this age it is doubtful that these infants knew or remembered that the mother was behind the cloth (they did not laugh at silent peekaboo or masked approach). Rather, this is probably laughter to a dynamic visual stimulus occurring against the background of excitation produced by mother calling the baby, then disappearing behind the cloth. Nonetheless, laughter to gentle jiggling and, especially, to approach-with-covered-face, indicates that it is no longer necessary to jog the infant with vigorous stimulation in order to produce laughter. The infant's participation has become greater; some of the tension now is produced by the infant's engagement of the stimulation.

In this small sample there was a striking change in the next two months, a veritable social explosion. The infants laughed at *many more items,* and the nature of the items eliciting laughter was dramatically changed. Seven-month-olds laughed at five of the seven social items and at three of the visual items, while continuing to laugh at several auditory and tactile items. They laughed, for example, at mother shaking her hair in front of

49

their faces and at mother approaching with cloth-covered face as well as at cloth-in-mouth and playing tug. The auditory (horse sound) and tactile (coochy-coo) items that they added were both very moderate in intensity, and laughter virtually always developed after several presentations. Again, we would point to the infant's increasing ability to discern patterning as well as his increased sociability. Seven months was the only age at which one-third of the infants laughed at their own reflection in the mirror. After seven months laughter dropped out, and coy observance developed in the mirror situation. The laughter at seven months probably reflects a social tendency (laughing at the infant they see), rather than self-recognition. Other evidence has shown that self-recognition does not occur until about fifteen to eighteen months (see Chapter 9).

One-third of the eight-month-olds laughed at (soundless) peekaboo, at pulling a dangling cloth from the mother's mouth, and at three visual items (mother crawling on floor, shaking her hair in the infant's face, and at having their own faces covered and uncovered). Like the seven-month-olds they showed a tendency to be influenced by dynamic stimulation because of the increasing capacity to follow stimulus change and to impose order on the sequence of stimulation.

As seen in Table 4-1, the trend toward laughter to subtle and complex visual and social stimulation continues through the remainder of the first year, with twelve-month-olds laughing at the greatest number of social and visual items. In addition to each of the items laughed at by eight-month-olds, they laughed at mother approaching-with-mask, sucking on the infant's bottle, walking "like a penguin," and sticking out her tongue (pulling it in as the infant reaches for it). Each of these subtle items has an obvious element of cognitive incongruity. It is no longer stimulation per se that elicits laughter, but now clearly it is an interaction of the situation with the baby's mental effort. The mother with the baby bottle in her mouth does not excite the five- or six-month-old infant, though it may watch this event carefully, with sober expression. The twelve-month-old must be excited not by the visual event but by its "interpretation" of the visual event.

As the trend toward laughter to these more sophisticated items was occurring in the second half-year, there was a parallel decline in the potency of physical stimulation items. As happened with smiling to faces or to repeated presentation of other visual stimuli these items became "old hat." There was not sufficient incongruity or subtlety to tax the infants' capacities. The situation could be assimilated or mastered readily. Thus, by eight months only one of the earlier effective intrusive items (kissing stomach) was successful. There was some revival in laughter to such items at the end of the first year, but at this time it was clear that the items had been transformed by the infant. For example, the oldest babies laughed *in anticipation* of being touched in "coochy-coo" or kissed in "kissing stomach." (Likewise the oldest infants laughed harder in stuffing the dangling cloth back into mother's mouth than they did at pulling it out; see Figure 2-1.)

As is the case with smiling in the first three months, there is a clear tendency for a progressively more active role for the infant in producing laughter. At first, laughter is in response to stimulation that intrudes. Then laughter occurs to situations requiring some degree of attention or some minimal "pattern recognition." Then situations in which the infant participates in producing the item become more potent (e.g., pulling the cloth from the mother's mouth) or that require sustained attention, and/or interpretation. The trend toward active participation continues, as in the older infant's attempt to stuff the cloth back into the mother's mouth and seeking to reproduce the situation. Infants in the second year have been observed to laugh harder when covering the adults' faces than when having their own faces covered.

Interpretation: Laughter, Tension, Cognitive Development

A great deal about the basic nature of the child's cognitive development, as well as its emotional growth, is revealed by smiling, laughter, and the relationship between them. As smiling reflects a tension–relaxation cycle, laughter—the maximal positive affect reaction—reflects a very sharp tension fluctuation. If this is so and if the developmental steps just described are accurate, there are clear implications concerning mental (cognitive) development. When the ten-month-old infant laughs at the caregiver sucking on the bottle, this reflects a rapid processing of incongruity, a cognitive production of a rapid tension fluctuation, build-up, and resolution. The six-month-old stares soberly at the bottle, though she or he clearly recognizes it and eventually may cry for it. But the ten-month-old laughs at this scene. She or he is not seeing just the bottle, or the mother and the bottle, but the mother *with* the bottle. In some way the idea of the mother is coordinated with the idea of the bottle. Though we cannot be certain of the infant's experience, its laughter implies that the baby in some sense grasps the incongruity.

Figure 4-3. A 16-month-old delights caregiver and herself by substituting a foot for part of her yogurt lunch. (Photo: G. Sroufe.)

This is a profound development. With his or her cognitive structures, the older infant is in some sense duplicating the internal tension state generated when the six-month-old was tickled, jiggled, or kissed on the stomach. This is truly a qualitative turn in development, fully comparable to what is witnessed in the first three months of life when the infant smiles at static visual displays.

Tension is a central concept in development. As I use the term, it is a natural consequence of the infant actively being engaged in a stimulus situation, with no necessary implication of anxiety or noxiousness (see Chapter 5). Tension may be thought of as mental effort, and such mental effort is as natural as breathing. It is a part of the infant's continuing experience.

Psychological development is viewed as an *active* process. Growth follows periods of disequilibrium, to use Piaget's term. Simply, this means that whenever the infant confronts a novel event he seeks to act on it in terms of existing mental structures. If it is easily incorporated (assimilated), his engagement is short-lived. Disequilibrium does not occur, but neither is there significant mental growth. (The business of simply exercising structures, however, is also an important part of development, as is discussed in Chapter 6.) When something does not fit, this produces disequilibrium *and effort to make it fit.* This is a basic assumption about the nature of the child as a *seeker.* From this effort, and a modification of the mental structures, equilibrium again is achieved. There is growth, because to accommodate to the nonfitting experience, the mental structures had to be broadened and made more precise.

From this description the interplay between emotional and cognitive factors should be clear. When confronting something novel, especially the familiar-yet-unfamiliar, the infant is motivated (curiosity, interest, mastery) to make it fit. As Piaget says, this is the "force" for cognitive growth. Through cognitive effort, a new fit (equilibrium) is achieved by modifying the mental structures. The disequilibrium–equilibrium (tension–relaxation) experience is pleasurable or joyful for the infant. Pleasure and joy are intrinsic in growth and mastery.

In this book there is so much emphasis on smiling and laughter because they touch basic aspects of development. Growth and mastery are pleasurable; your infant naturally seeks to grow, to incorporate its environment, and to fit itself to its experience. You should know this more than any other fact about development. You will know it as you watch and interact with your baby, as you and your baby smile and laugh together.

Some Evidence for the Role
of Tension in Laughter

Since tension is so central to the interpretation of laughter, in this section and the next some explicit evidence for its role is presented. The relationship between crying (fear) and laughter to the same item was mentioned earlier and is discussed in the next chapter. Another clear bit of evidence concerning the tension-fluctuation notion is the special potency of items that build to a climax with an abrupt cutoff (for example, "Gonna Getchu," the swelling "Aah"). If the swelling "Aah" (which becomes louder and louder, then is cut off abruptly is not swelled and abruptly cut off but rather is swelled and then tapered ($\frown$ vs $\frown$), it is not very effective in producing laughter. The focused terminal point promotes a rapid drop in tension following an acute increase.

Results with repeated presentations of the laughter items offer additional evidence for the role of tension and cognitive processes in laughter. As smiling sometimes develops from a sober expression on initial presentations of an event, laughter frequently builds from smiling. The ten-month-old infant might merely do a double take and watch with rapt attention the first time the mother pretends to suck on the bottle. A tiny, often quizzical smile may appear at the end of the presentation, or the infant may smile on the second presentation. The exact pattern varies from infant to infant and situation to situation. There may be several episodes of neutral or smile expressions, but laughter commonly builds from neutral, smiling, and active (vigorous) smiling reactions on initial presentations; it frequently fades again to smiling after several repetitions.

You will not see a series of presentations with the infant laughing, then neutral, then laughing (unless he did not pay attention on Trial 2); or laughing, crying, smiling, laughing; or even very often laughing, smiling, laughing. The magnitude of the positive affective reaction builds, then wanes; and this provides an important clue about speed of processing and tension fluctuation in laughter. It makes sense that laughter, a stronger affective release, would require a faster increase in tension and faster resolution (a sharper "tension jag") than smiling. It also makes sense that with repeated exposure to the situation, the incongruity could be "grasped" and resolved more rapidly. And one would expect some carry-over of engagement (excitation and tension) from the previous exposures. Tension level is high, and the tension fluctuation is rapid; so laughter results.

The return to smiling is not because the infant no longer can resolve the incongruity quickly but because engagement (tension) declines. Ultimately of course, the infant will become disinterested in most events if they simply are repeated. *That is why when you are engaged in face-to-face play with your baby you continually vary your expression, vocalizations, and movements. You maintain its tension level, its engagement.*

Smiling and Laughter with Down's Syndrome Infants

Much of what has been said about the role of tension in laughter and about the close ties between cognitive development and affective expression is revealed most clearly in our studies of infants with

Down's syndrome (mongolism).[2] The most basic finding, of course, is that fundamentally the same integrated process is found. Cognitive development is reflected reliably in affective growth; emotional and cognitive development proceed side by side in an interlocking manner. Retarded infants develop, too. And their development is intricate and complex.

Our initial study involved twenty-four infants with Down's syndrome. There were great individual differences among these babies. Like other Down's syndrome infants, it can be expected that some of them will approach normal ability; others will be retarded rather seriously. We were interested in seeing whether development as an integrated process could be shown with these babies and whether their obvious hypotonia (lack of muscle tone) would have consequences for (be associated with) affective expression. Therefore, we saw these babies monthly, most beginning at age four months, until age sixteen months. We saw them several more times up to age two years. At each point we gathered data on smiling and laughter in our standard situations. We also tested mental and motor development with two standard instruments, the Bayley test and the Uzgiris–Hunt Scales. With some babies fear reactions also were assessed in standard laboratory situations.

Most normal babies begin laughing by age four months, but these infants did not laugh, on the average, until age nine months. The three most hypotonic (muscularly flaccid) infants began laughing after age thirteen months. Laughing later than

[2]Cicchetti, D., & Sroufe, L. A. The emotional development of the infant with Down's syndrome. In J. L. Poor & E. A. Davis (Eds.), *Aim to fight low expectation of Down's syndrome children.* Forest Lake, MN: Forest Lake Printing, 1976, 37–59.

age four months certainly does *not* indicate that an individual baby is retarded, but group data like these clearly reflect the slow development of Down's syndrome infants.

Other findings were much more important than this age-of-onset result. Although Down's babies laughed later, they laughed at the items in roughly *the same order* as the normal infants; that is, they laughed at the physically intrusive items first and at the more subtle items much later. Both the delayed onset and the long delay to laugh at the visual items reflect their retardation. Most significantly, Down's infants *smiled* at items in the *order* normal babies *laugh;* that is, even when there was evidence that there was some comprehension of the item (reflected in differential smiling), Down's infants did not laugh. In terms of our position the conclusion is obvious: either the infants did not generate a comparable amount of tension, or they could not process the incongruity with sufficient speed to produce the "tension jag" required for laughter, only at the speed required for smiling.

Comparisons with the mental tests confirmed our ideas about laughter and smiling keeping pace with cognitive development. The babies with the highest test scores were consistently those smiling and laughing at the more sophisticated items. And when older Down's and younger normal infants were matched in terms of mental scores, they were also very similar in terms of affective expression.

I have included this section, because this study illustrates quite well some of the principles we have been discussing. Development is an integrated process. Emotional and cognitive factors are linked closely. Laughter reflects the tension of engagement and rapid cognitive processing. But you must not view our laughter situations, or your observations on smiling, as a test of whether your child is intellectually normal. Failure to laugh at four months or never laughing at some of our items in no way suggests a child is retarded intellectually. It is equally unwise to conclude that your infant is gifted, based on smiling and laughter. It just does not work that way. Children smile or laugh or do not smile or laugh for a variety of reasons, especially with regard to particular items. You see, in a sense we stacked the deck by selecting a *group* of infants we knew would be retarded and then looking for the affective associates. The implication for you and your baby is to confirm again your intuition that your baby's development is complex, intricate, organized. Like you, parents of these Down's symdrome babies were amazed at their infant's remarkable development. All babies are fascinating; all babies exhibit intelligence. Intelligence is a natural aspect of human development.

Summary and Integration

With the smiles of recognition or mastery we suggested that the tension was the result of the infant's *efforts* to bring the novel stimulus event into harmony with internalized models (schemes) of events. When this cannot be done, the infant modifies his mental structures so that unless the event is beyond his grasp, he ultimately will be able to fit it (assimilate it) into his internal model. This ''matching'' process requires mental effort, however, and therefore creates tension. With assimilation of some portion of the event (some matching), there is also relaxation. The smile is an aspect of that relaxation process.

Laughter represents a faster bringing into harmony of the discrepant event, overcoming greater disequilibrium, assimilating (fitting in) a greater portion of the discrepant event, and/or a high level of background tension. The building of laughter from smiling over trials, in addition to reflecting more rapid processing with experience, also suggests greater engagement (therefore tension) with repeated exposure. This again implies a very active interaction between the infant and its experience. As the infant is exposed to a novel situation, he or she becomes better able to invest herself or himself in it.

Another way of conceptualizing the younger infant's failure to smile or laugh at an item such as mother-approaching-with-mask is not that he fails to assimilate this situation but rather that he assimilates it to a very primitive and broad scheme. The baby has learned to reach for (and mouth) anything and everything he sees (a sensory–motor scheme). The brightly colored mask captures its attention, and the baby readily assimilates it to its reaching scheme without effort. The older infant's failure to smile on early presentations of the mask is for a very different reason: the baby is not able to assimilate the novel event, because he or she is attempting to impose more sophisticated, advanced structures on it. In fitting himself to this novel event by modifying his models (overcoming the disequilibrium), the ten-month-old is achieving significant growth. This growth, however, is dependent on the groundwork established earlier by repeated experiences with established structures. According to Piaget, models or schemes must be consolidated well before they can be modified and reorganized in a more complex way. Thus, the

practicing behavior discussed in Chapter 6 is also

highly relevant to cognitive growth. It is the repetition and overextension of the established structures that lead to conflict with reality, disequilibrium, and modification. Again, the infant's smiling and laughter are major clues to these important developments and to the operation of the disequilibrium-accommodation-assimilation process. Important things are happening when your baby smiles and laughs, and there is pleasure and joy in active mastery.

Sources

BERLYNE, D. E. Laughter, humor and play. In G. Lindzey & E. Aronson (Eds.), *Handbook of social psychology (2nd ed., Vol. 3)*. Boston: Addison-Wesley, 1969.

CICCHETTI, D., & SROUFE, L. A. The relationship between affective and cognitive development in Down's syndrome infants. *Child Development,* 1976, *47,* 920–29.

CICCHETTI, D., & SROUFE, L. A. The emotional development of the infant with Down's syndrome. In J. L. Poor & E. A. Davis (Eds.), *Aim to fight low expectation of Down's syndrome children.* Forest Lake, MN: Forest Lake Printing, 1976, 37–59.

FLAVELL, J. H. *The developmental psychology of Jean Piaget.* New York: Van Nostrand Reinhold Company, 1963.

SROUFE, L. A., & WATERS, E. The ontogenesis of smiling and laughter: A perspective on the organization of development in infancy. *Psychological Review,* 1976, *83,* 173–89.

SROUFE, L. A., & WUNSCH, J. P. The development of laughter in the first year of life. *Child Development,* 1972, *43,* 1326–44.

5

Joy, Fear, & the Unfamiliar: The Role of Your Relationship

. . . The same kinds of situations reported to produce fear are the most potent for releasing laughter . . . In general, the more secure the context, the less likely the infant is to be afraid and the more likely there will be smiling and laughter in the face of novelty or incongruity.

Even if you were persuaded by what was said in the last chapter, you still may be having trouble with the idea that disequilibrium or what we are calling tension would always be associated with pleasure. In fact, of course, it is not. Disequilibrium, "not fitting," and uncertainty can at times produce distress; and well-known psychologists have suggested that such factors are responsible for the experience of fear. How is it then that disequilibrium sometimes can lead to distress or fear and sometimes lead to pleasure?

One ingredient you may have thought of already is whether the infant is able to overcome the disequilibrium, to change his mental structures so the discrepant event does fit. This is consistent with the examples in the preceding chapter, in which smiling and laughter were seen following accommodation to the novel event. But beyond the amount of discrepancy of an event from the child's "model," and even beyond resolution of the disequilibrium, there is another factor determining whether the infant will experience fear or joy in the face of "mental shake-up." In our work we refer to this factor as *security of context*.

Consider two examples. A ten-month-old infant is sitting in a highchair in a hallway at the University of Minnesota. His mother is just inside the room, filling out a form, but he is not watching her. He is playing with a toy on the tray, apparently contented. I step out of a nearby room and call the infant's name. When the infant looks up, I present a brightly colored, human-looking mask. I slowly cover my face with the mask, step toward the baby, and lean to within about a foot of the baby's face. Because we do not like to frighten babies, I have done this exact procedure only three times (though we have done masked approaches many times with the baby in its mother's presence). In each of these three cases the reaction was the same. At first the baby became completely still, frozen. It watched with unswerving glance. As I moved forward, the motionless expression changed to a pucker, then a cry with the head turning completely away. (Recordings in our laboratory show that the heart rate would be speeding up dramatically at the end of my approach.)

The reaction of these three infants is in stark contrast to what we have observed in our studies of laughter in the home. We use the *very same mask*. But in the playful, home context, with the mother putting on the mask in the infant's view, no ten-month-old infant has *ever* cried. With dozens of infants tested, *smiling was universal,* and about half *laughed* in response to the masked

63

approach situation. The same mask can produce distress or laughter.

Discrepancy or incongruity is clearly important in each of these masked approach situations. The situation is salient, because it involves a transformation of the mother's or stranger's face; it is challenging to the older infant because the person changes, yet is the same. This is a situation that clearly would produce disequilibrium, or tension, *in both cases.* If you looked at films of these two situations, you would not be able to predict the baby's reaction from his initial response. With mother *or* stranger, the baby first stops everything and looks intently. Tension develops. In one case, however, the tension results in smiling, probably followed by reaching. In the other case, it is associated with crying and avoidance. To help make this state of affairs understandable, I would like to share with you our work on the importance of context in determining infant behavior.[1]

Our work on the relationship of joy and fear to context began with the observation that *in general the same kinds of situations reported to produce fear were the most potent for releasing laughter.* Loss of balance and loud sounds once were thought of as the major, inborn elicitors of fear, and masks have been reported to produce fear widely. In the home, however, in play with the caregiver, such situations routinely produce a great deal of smiling and laughter. With young infants, "Boom boom boom" and jiggling the baby are excellent laughter items, as are tossing the baby into the air or dropping it between your knees at a somewhat later age. With older infants, when the

---

[1]Sroufe, L. A., Waters, E., & Matas, L. Contextual determinants of infant affective response. In M. Lewis & L. Rosenblum (Eds.), *The origins of fear.* New York: John Wiley and Sons, Inc., 1974.

mask becomes capable of producing fear, *it is also a potent laughter stimulus.* This makes sense if one assumes that tension (disequilibrium) is necessary for both distress and laughter.

We next did a series of studies explicitly concerned with context. We found, for example, that even when the *mother* put on the mask we had used in the homes, there was virtually *no laughter in the laboratory,* though half had laughed in the home. Many of the infants still smiled in the laboratory, but if the observations were made *following a brief separation* from the mother, even smiling was reduced. Also, if a stranger put on the mask first and then the mother, the baby was less likely to smile at the mother with mask. Some even cried. When the mother preceded the stranger, infants tended to be more positive in their reactions to the stranger. Finally, in our studies of reactions to approaching strangers (without a mask) we found that babies showed more fear in the laboratory than at home and showed less fear in the laboratory if given time to become familiar with their surroundings. *In general, the more secure the context, the less likely the infant is to be afraid and the more likely there will be smiling and laughter in the face of novelty or incongruity.*

These statements about context, of course, do not apply to all babies on any day. Some babies do not smile very often even when in a positive context; others are generally jovial. Babies differ in temperament and have fluctuations in mood just like the rest of us! One day a baby may be moody and irritable, and it will be less likely to smile and more likely to get upset. On another day the same infant may smile, laugh, and play a great deal. It even has been our experience with older babies (say ten months) that mere contact with the experimenters in the laboratory is upsetting after a visit to the doctor for a shot.

Still, in general the statements about context tend to hold. Infants, by the time they are about eight to ten months old, generally are more wary and less positive in an unfamiliar situation in the absence of their caregiver or following some other upsetting event. Even giving them some time to become familiar with a new situation makes a vast difference in their reactivity. Up through age six months, context does not have such noticeable effects, though it is probably never irrelevant.

The main conclusion to be reached from this information concerning the powerful influence of context is that the infant's motivation concerning the unfamiliar is incredibly complex. The question has been asked, do infants seek to approach novelty or avoid it? (Are they affiliative toward or wary of strange persons?) From our evidence the answer is clearly, both. Both the tendency to approach and the tendency to avoid (be afraid of) novelty are quite strong. Disequilibrium in the face of incongruity may attract or repel the infant or both. Infants often avert their eyes from approaching strangers and sometimes turn completely away or cry. But they also offer them toys, watch them carefully, and smile at them when they are still across the room. Infants are sometimes cautious in a new situation, but often they are exploring it quickly with enthusiasm. It is this complex motivation concerning the unfamiliar that is the focus of this chapter, and it is also the key to understanding the relationship between fear and joy, the importance of smiling and laughter, and the meaning of tension. Ultimately, all of this illustrates a clear way in which the caregiver–infant relationship is important to the infant's development.

Motivation Concerning the Unfamiliar:
The Function of Smiling

In our work we adopt the adaptational viewpoint. This has two aspects. First, we assume that such infant behaviors as the smile are meaningful; they serve some function for the infant. Behaviors are not random but rather are organized with respect to adaptive functioning. Second, behavior is viewed within its evolutionary context, in terms of individual and species survival.

From an adaptational viewpoint it is easy to see why novel events must hold an attraction for the human infant. The greatest survival advantage of our species has been our flexible use of the environment. We are opportunists, whose livelihood and well-being have depended upon seeing new combinations and twists on what was already familiar. Mastery of novel situations, even when not immediately useful, has long-term consequences for such a being. What begins as a satisfaction of curiosity later may have great utility. And, as discussed in Chapters 3 and 4, cognitive growth goes forward because existing structures are modified in the face of novel experiences. Curiosity and mastery are two strong motives that are aroused by novel stimulation.

But novel stimulation also calls forth avoidance and wary motives. As ethological theorist John Bowlby has suggested, something you do not know may harm you, and harm is more likely in an unfamiliar setting. As children now may get hurt by touching a brightly colored pin, once they may have been prey for panthers and other large cats if they wandered from the safety of home. It also seems likely that not being able to make sense out of a novel situation inherently could be tied to an experience of threat and discomfort. It certainly involves effort to try, and effort without completion may be unpleasant.

As Louis Breger has written, there is curiosity about the unfamiliar, but there is security in what is known. This motivational duality is perhaps the fundamental aspect of development. The novel, the unfamiliar, the incongruous calls the infant forward; but the comfort and security of what is familiar bids him to stay. Ideally, curiosity, exploratory, and mastery motivation is dominant but in balance with some tendency to be cautious. Research confirms this as the normative pattern. By about nine months, infants at first will be hesitant upon presentation of a novel object. They will inspect it. Then, in mother's presence they will reach for it. Younger babies immediately reach.[2]

The salience of novel situations also is confirmed by the infant's reaction to our situations. When the mask is presented, the mother sucks on the infant's bottle, the stranger appears at the door, or virtually any new stimulus is encountered, the infant ceases ongoing activity, even sucking on a bottle. It stills completely and fixes its gaze on the object. This reaction is observed readily, as in our earlier examples. A host of internal changes also occurs (heart rate slowing, blood flow changes, alteration of brain wave patterns, and so on) that have the effect of increasing the infant's sensitivity to stimulation.

This complex reaction (called the *orienting response*) is vital if the infant is to process information efficiently. It is important that distracting activity cease and that the infant focus completely on the novel event. But it is equally important that

68   [2]Schaffer, Greenwood, & Parry, 1972.

the infant be able to complete this orienting phase and act with respect to the situation, either approaching it or avoiding it. This is where the expression of affect comes in. This is where the functional significance of smiling and laughter becomes clear. We are complex beings, and our reactions to novelty reflect that complexity.

It is during the orienting phase that tension develops. Engaging the novel event, with the investment of cognitive effort and inhibition of activity, leads to an increase in tension. In some instances, especially where the engagement is modest, this tension probably simply can dissipate. More likely, if the infant is engaged strongly, it can be *released* through affective expression.

The infant may cry and turn from the stimulus or simply avoid it, or it may smile or laugh. Though the tension may be released with either positive (smiling, laughter) or negative (crying, avoidance) affect, these two modes of expression have very different consequences.

Crying involves first a sharp increase in arousal and later a fatigue reaction when the infant is comforted or simply exhausted. Crying and avoidance, however, have the consequence of taking the infant away from the situation. And until the end of the first year, crying is a rather total response. The infant tends to become locked into it in an "all-or-none" fashion, unable to stop. A ten-month-old infant who cries on the first presentation of the mask virtually always cries and turns away *sooner* on the second presentation. Clearly, this reaction is incompatible with resolving the disequilibrium. The avoiding infant does not continue to stay engaged with the event and so will not get accustomed to it; or, in Piaget's terms, he will not be able to assimilate it. His cognitive structures **69** will not be expanded. Nonetheless, crying is a perfectly natural reaction when the level of tension is too high, when it exceeds some critical threshold. Crying is a signal of distress, a reaction to high and sustained tension. The avoidance pattern and even crying, in a sense, removes the infant from the situation.

Smiling is also an expression of tension, associated with relaxation of tension. *When positive affect is associated with tension release, however, the infant stays oriented toward the situation,* in fact often seeking to reproduce it. If the infant smiles (and reaches) for the mask on the first presentation, he or she is likely to smile and reach *sooner* on the second approach. Engagement of the incongruous event is maintained, and ultimately the infant is able to broaden his or her cognitive structures to make room for it. Smiling may not mean that the disequilibrium is resolved; it may rather be a part of the assimilation process. *Smiling is a means the baby has for releasing or modulating tension* (keeping it at a modest level) *so that it resolves the disequilibrium.*

A related function of the smile may be to overcome the inhibition of the orienting phase. The infant is frozen, locked into the event. With crying it turns away, but with smiling it stays oriented toward the mask and approaches it. In this situation, with a discretely presented novel event, the sequence is always smile, *then* reach, or smile *and* reach. It is never reach, *then* smile. The smile seems to release the reach. When the tension and inhibition of the orienting reaction is released, the infant can act. So the smile promotes action and continued commerce with the novel situation. As a signal of pleasure to the caregiver, it also encourages repetition of the event, providing further opportunities for assimilation.

The Role of the Relationship:
Attachment

Now for a central point: The tendency to approach, struggle with, accommodate to, and, finally, master novel experiences does not exist in a given amount. The amount of tension that can be tolerated varies. It clearly differs from situation to situation for the same baby, and it seems reasonable that it also varies from infant to infant. Our work has shown that infants are able to deal with novel experiences better if they are in a secure context. The work also has shown that a great deal of that security is tied to the caregiver. For groups of babies, mere presence of the caregiver has been shown to be a powerful factor. When the caregiver is present, infants are able to engage, approach, and stay in contact with novel experiences better. I believe also that the *quality* of the ongoing, caregiver–infant relationship is of great importance to the infant's sense of security.

Attachment is a concept that has become prominent in developmental psychology in recent years. Primarily, the term refers to the special intimacy and closeness between caregiver and infant. Attachment, familiarity, and security are tied together closely. The infant feels comfortable and secure with the caregiver because she or he is familiar. The caregiver is what is known, and the infant ventures out into the unknown from this base, returning for contact or comforting when necessary.

Mary Ainsworth has defined *attachment* in terms of its balance with exploration. The securely attached infant can explore its surroundings, because it can use the caregiver as a base, with ever more tolerance for separation as development occurs. The knowability of the caregiver is a bit of familiarity

that the infant can take along into a novel experience, much as the toddler will carry its blanket. In
a new situation the caregiver's presence is often
sufficient. Sometimes periods of actual physical
closeness will be required, or even physical comforting, but the securely attached infant can use its
caregiver as a secure base from which to explore
its environment. From this view of attachment,
the optimally functioning (securely attached) infant
is not the one who always is clinging to the caregiver or the one who never seeks contact, even
when it needs it. The securely attached infant is
the one who can move out from the caregiver when
external stress is minimal (Figure 5-1) but who
reestablishes contact under stressful conditions. It
is "securely" attached precisely because it is completely confident that the comforting will be there
when it needs it. It can venture into the unknown,
resting in this knowledge. Knowledge at this age
is, of course, much more a feeling than anything
else. It is a feeling of security that derives from
the reliability of the caregiver as a source of comforting and harmonious interchange.

All of this is very important. It is important
that infants be able to explore new aspects of their
world. There is joy in discovery and mastery.
Growth itself is of value, and growth derives from
approaching and mastering novel experiences. If
excessive timidity and wariness prevent the infant
from exploring its available environment when it
is not objectively harmful, this limits growth.
Again, wariness concerning the unfamiliar is not
unhealthy. Neither is the tendency to seek proximity
and comforting from the caregiver when frightened
or distressed. It is natural, normal, . . . expected.
It is only unhealthy if these tendencies are so strong
that the countertendency to approach and explore

is submerged. All infants will at times be frightened by novel or unusual experiences. This is only a serious problem if they cannot be comforted, cannot draw sufficient security from their attachment relationships, if wariness therefore becomes a general approach to life.

Figure 5-1. This infant plays happily while the caregiver is nearby. Note that the toy is the wastebasket. (Photo: P. LaSota.)

To be sure, a great deal of development occurs simply in the face of maturation and experience. But there is no question about the importance of the caregiver–infant relationship in shaping that development. The infant's style in approaching its experience is as important as specific developmental achievements. An enthusiasm for experience, a curiosity about novel events, and a sense of joy in mastery are part of any definition of adequate cognitive functioning. And the relationship you have with the infant in your care can foster such characteristics.

What then is the basis for a secure, vital, **73**

attachment relationship? How can it be insured that your infant will be able to draw on your relationship as an aid in approaching incongruity and as a base for retreat when necessary? How can your relationship be developed to support your infant's emotional and cognitive growth?

The most basic answer is, of course, that a strong attachment relationship between you and your baby will probably develop in the natural course of events. You love your baby. You are interested in your baby. There is enough stability in its physical world and enough change that familiarity and novelty are both available.

Other things also can be said in answer to this basic question from work in child psychology. Warmth and physical contact are clearly important. Being with your baby, being close to your baby, handling your baby—all of these will contribute to your familiarity. More abstract qualities of caregiver behavior are important as well. These qualities have been described with terms such as *sensitivity, responsivity, mutuality, reciprocity,* and *cooperativeness.* These concepts overlap a great deal, all referring in some way to a reliability and dependability of input from you, without intrusiveness.

Being *sensitive* means being *responsive* to the infant's signals, knowing the language of the baby's behavior, and responding to its cues. The young infant's cry, for example, is a signal of distress. In the early months, the baby is not crying to manipulate *you,* to express anger at you, or because you are spoiling it. Its cry signals distress, much like shivering signals cold. Viewing crying as a signal, you obviously want to respond to it as consistently as possible, though of course you cannot always, nor do you need to. You have your needs, as do others in your family. But the sensitive caregiver responds as often, as soon, and as effectively as possible, terminating the source of distress.

In an important study by Bell and Ainsworth, it was found that when mothers picked up young babies quite soon when they cried, these babies were crying *less* by the end of the first year than was a group who was responded to more slowly or not at all. The babies *were not spoiled* by being picked up, though this is of course possible with older babies and toddlers. Rather, these babies seemed to have learned a sense of security, that is, that the caregiver is responsive. By the end of the first year, they "knew" they would be comforted when they needed it and probably could rely on other kinds of signals as well. Responding reliably to the infant's signals is an important part of its security.

Responsivity, mutuality, reciprocity, and co-operativeness all are related. When you respond to your baby's signals, you lay the groundwork for a sense of potency. The infant finds that the world (caregiver) responds to its needs; the infant can have an effect. Likewise, such a sense is fostered when you tune your ministrations to the infant's activity. The baby is stimulated when it is *open* to stimulation. Stimulation and baby-initiated actions are not at cross-purposes. They are blended. There is a flow in the interaction, with smooth transitions between activities. You do not, for example, just jerk your infant away from a toy and plunk him into the bath. You get his attention on you and your voice and face. To this stimulation you may add some water play—maybe by wiping gently with a lukewarm cloth. Then, gradually, the bath. The infant learns that stimulation from you (in the context of you) is not chaotic, is not strident. Although during early infancy mutuality and reciprocity refer primarily to *your* consistency and reliability (your making room for the infant's needs), the sense of trust and effectance that comes out of noncapriciousness ultimately will promote a truly mutual interaction.

How does one learn all of this—to be sensitive to the infant's signals, to be responsive to its moods, and to cooperate with its actions? Basically, your baby will teach you. You will learn your baby's signal system, and you will learn about its needs and preferences through interaction. You will learn by being with and playing with your baby, by enjoying your baby. As you learn the individual nature of your baby and learn to respond to its needs effectively, you will feel secure about your caregiving. The infant will respond to your caregiving. Your ways and style will become familiar to the infant. You will build familiarity and security together. Within such a secure relationship, you promote your infant's exploration and mastery of the social and nonsocial environment.

Sources

AINSWORTH, M., & BELL, S. Mother–infant interaction and the development of competence. In K. Connolly & J. Bruner (Eds.), *The growth of competence.* London: Academic Press, 1973, 97–118.

BELL, S., & AINSWORTH, M. Infant crying and maternal responsiveness. *Child Development,* 1972, *43,* 1171–90.

BREGER, L. *From instinct to identity: The development of personality.* Englewood Cliffs, N.J.: Prentice-Hall, Inc., 1974.

BOWLBY, J. *Attachment and loss. Vol. 1. Attachment.* New York: Basic Books, 1969.

BOWLBY, J. *Attachment and loss. Vol. 2. Separation: Anxiety and anger.* New York: Basic Books, 1973.

SCHAFFER, H., GREENWOOD, A., & PARRY, M. The onset of wariness. *Child Development,* 1972, *43,* 165–75.

SROUFE, L., & WATERS, E. The ontogenesis of smiling and laughter: A perspective on the organization of development in infancy. *Psychological Review,* 1976, *83,* 173–89.

SROUFE, L. A., WATERS, E., & MATAS, L. Contextual determinants of infant affective response. In M. Lewis & L. Rosenblum (Eds.), *The origins of fear.* New York: John Wiley and Sons, Inc., 1974.

6

The Infant
at Play

*The mother tends to provide a "holding" framework
for her own cues. That is, she holds the infant with
her hands, with her eyes, with her voice and smile, and
with changes from one modality to another as he habitu-
ates to one or another. All these holding experiences are
opportunities for the infant to learn how to contain*
himself, *how to control motor responses, and how to
attend for longer and longer periods. They amount to a
kind of learning about organization of behavior in
order to attend.*

BRAZELTON, KOSLOWSKI, AND MAIN, *The Origins of
Reciprocity*

In the life of the infant there is no separation
between learning and play. Expansion of the infant's cognitive abilities is a by-product of play;
it derives from the exploration and manipulation
of objects in the environment and from repetition
of actions with no apparent purpose. Play is the
infant's realm.

When the biological needs for sleep, feeding,
and elimination of discomfort are met, the infant
continually is taking in psychological nourishment.
78 The awake infant is exploring the surroundings

with its senses and with its hands and mouth constantly. As anyone who lives with an infant knows,
it is not long before even feeding becomes a time
for play, and crying from discomfort can be elimi-
nated temporarily by interesting sights or sounds or
by presentation of an object to manipulate. Watching infants makes it completely clear that they do
not seek simply relief from tension. When their
physiological needs are met, they constantly are
seeking psychological stimulation.

Piaget has spoken of the "need to function,"
"overassimilation," and "exercising schemes."
All these terms refer to the infant's natural tendency
to exercise its abilities, to do what it can with the
social and physical environment; that is, to explore
it and play with it. Thus, the two-month-old constantly explores the surroundings with its eyes
when it is contented. The five-month-old grasps
and mouths virtually every object encountered and
in this way exercises its particular capacities for
exploring and knowing its world. Through such
encounters the infant learns to distinguish the body
from the nonbody and learns about the many
properties of objects.

The very process of psychological development itself is based on play. The organization of
acts into more complex units was one of the fundamental characteristics of development discussed in
Chapter 2. When the ten-month-old infant smiles,
reaches up his or her arms, and vocalizes as the
caregiver approaches, we speak of "greeting behavior." Each of these subcapacities existed much
earlier than the organized greeting made its appearance. And each was engaged in many times as
separate behavior, for example, the baby extending
its arms when being picked up. Similarly, when the
infant learns to stand up in the middle of the room
and walk, it draws on a history of skill at rising **79**

from its knees to its hands and toes (with arms and legs straight and rump in air), standing with the aid of furniture, and maintaining balance with the help of an adult hand. Each of these subacts was practiced repeatedly, often for several weeks. Over and over again the infant pulls himself or herself up to a stand by the couch, sits, and stands again. Especially when such skills are first "invented" the infant can be seen to engage in the act over and over, despite occasionally frustrating results. Since infants are just as likely (perhaps even more so) to practice when they are unaware of adult presence, it is clear that such actions must be inherently rewarding. And the smiles and laughter that accompany these repetitive activities testify to this (see Figures 6-1 and 7-4). Such practice is play.

Putting together actions, for example the components of standing and walking, sometimes may be motivated by the goal of being like adults or siblings (though such an idea raises the interesting question of why infants would want to be like others). Increasingly during the first year, it makes sense to think of infants as having intentions and goals in the sense we use such terms (see Chapter 8). But as one examines many subcomponents of later behaviors, it becomes hard to believe anything other than "babies do things they can do." Babies lift their heads and look around and in that way widen their world, but they also push to their hands and toes, bang a spoon on a tray, or roll over repeatedly, *simply to do it*. Such actions, which are done repeatedly, meet no physiological need. They require no external reward.

In putting behaviors together into the complex act, it seems that some critical mass of experience is required. The subcomponents are well mastered. Everyone knows the baby could walk; a few steps were seen when, unknown to the baby, the caregiver released the hand and the infant walked to the couch. Then one day the infant stands up in the middle of the floor, and WALKS. Walking with joy is common thereafter. The "idea" derives

Figure 6-1. This 7-month-old is enjoying simply pushing herself up to her hands and toes, a new skill that she repeats many times in the day. (Photo: David Morris.)

from the complete mastery of the subcomponents through repetition, through *play.* The infant's joy in doing, in mastery, is thus the psychological foundation for development, just as maturation is the physical foundation. Without the intrinsic reward in doing, the infant would not make the leap to the integrated behavior so soon. By repeating actions over and over in play, the subskills become completely mastered, so that concentration can be directed to the integration of the actions, to the total act.

The intrinsic motivation to do and to experience is at the base of the infant's intrapsychic (personality) development and social growth as well as the development of motor and object skill.

The capacities to tolerate tension and to sustain engagement with you and others in its social world rest on this motivation. Your knowledge of this motivation and cues from the infant will guide your interaction as you contribute to your infant's development through play. With sensitivity you can build on this intrinsic motivation without straining or stifling it. You will learn to cooperate with your infant in the process, and this will involve participating with him or her as well as allowing the infant the necessary space for mastery. You need not be concerned about motivating your baby to develop. That motivation is within the infant. But you have a clear role to play.

Caregiver and Infant at Play

Berry Brazelton, a pediatrician and careful observer of infants, has described the intricate social dance that occurs between the infant and a sensitive caregiver. The caregiver captures the infant's attention with soft tones, then holds its attention with changing facial expression and modulating voice, perhaps as in the following scenario: "Hello der you little debol . . . Mommy's gonna get you. Yes she is. (Brief pause.) Momma's gonna get you and gobble you right up. What do you think of that? (Brief pause.) Come on. Come on, you little dickens. Let me see those gums. Humm? (Pause.) Yeah, that's right . . . that's right. (Big smile, nodding head, and mother responds in kind.) Oh, well now, are you gonna say somethin'? Are ya? (Pause, mother nodding head, widening eyes.) Come on! (Pause, the baby begins cycling movements of the arms and kicking the feet.) Come on. (Drawn out, then longer pause.) Yeah!" (Mother laughs at the baby's gurgling sound.)

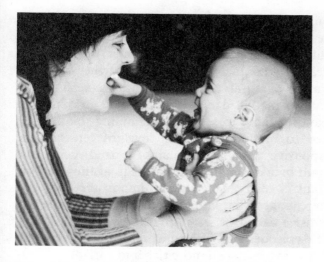

Figure 6-2. Caregiver and 6-month-old at play (Photo: Hunt Greene).

Brazelton describes the way the mother appropriately escalates and de-escalates the level of tension in the course of such an interaction. The infant is captured with gentle tones, and then the mother adds more stimulation with her nodding head, changing facial expressions, and voice, so that the infant stays attracted and his excitement builds. No facial expression or voice quality, unchanging, will maintain an infant's attention. But modulated tones and expression can build excitement (Figure 6-2). In fact, of course, at any age a baby can become overstimulated, overexcited. It is here that the sensitive caregiver takes cues from the baby. Babies will turn away, look away, or begin to show distress when the level of tension becomes too high. The sensitive response when the infant withdraws or becomes distressed in this situation is to de-escalate, to back off. The infant sometimes needs opportunities to rest and "regroup" before pushing on. Relax. Let the infant come to you. The infant is not rejecting you, and the excitement can be reestablished as it was initially. Pursuing the infant when it is seeking to break off contact will result in further attempts to avoid parental stimulation, or distress.

When this dance is done well, it is truly a beautiful thing to see. Understanding the infant's need to modulate its own level of tension, the responsive caregiver remains relaxed when the infant breaks contact and comes in again when the infant is ready. Sensing the importance of such interchanges, or simply *enjoying* them, the responsive caregiver stays involved with the infant, with episodes and the total encounter becoming greater in length and more rich and varied.

The infant derives a great deal from this play. In such play the roots of mutuality are set out. The infant gains a primitive sense of give and take, of social participation, and of effectance. The caregiver partner *will respond to him or her* as well as be a source of stimulation. The give and take is what takes the infant beyond imitation to a sense of true mutuality. Its action has an effect on you, and what you do in response to it further stimulates the infant to behave; and so it goes with each partner deriving a sense of participation. Likewise, the sense of timing and pacing is something that comes from the two of you. These are the notions psychologists have in mind when they speak of the sense of trust emerging from the infancy period. It comes from a reliability, a harmony, a non-intrusiveness of care.

The infant also learns to tolerate increasing amounts of tension through this interactive play, to hold himself as he is being "held" by the caregiver within the bonds of the interaction. As he can tolerate more tension without breaking contact and without his behavior becoming disorganized, the variety of situations (or sheer amount of stimulation) that can be engaged becomes expanded. Increasingly, the infant is not restricted to situations of moderate intensity, novelty, or complexity but can cope with an increasingly rich and varied experience. Tension tolerance and sustained attention in the face of challenging complexity are obvious foundations of important transactions with the environment and important learning. Infants and children learn through doing, through action. An increasing ability to maintain organized action in the face of complexity and novelty is of fundamental importance.

The caregiver in the scenario above actually helped the infant to organize its action both by building and maintaining his level of excitement and by allowing the infant room to make its response. The infant visually becomes excited, with smiles and bobbing head and with slow and then faster cycling movements of the arms and kicking of the feet. With appropriate timing of voice changes and changes in facial expression, the mother helps him build to the peak of tension ("come on, come on"), then pauses, and the gurgling sound from the baby spills forth.

Had the mother kept building the excitement, she may well have lost the baby. The infant may have laughed or turned away or, if the tension were too great, become distressed. If she had kept building the excitement, the organized vocal behavior would not have appeared. Unless the mother allows the infant space to respond, unless she *stops* talking, the infant has no room for participation (not unlike problems with some adult conversations!). As it is, this infant was helped to participate and to participate on an advanced level. Having made its gurgling response, the mother reacts with joyful vocalizations of her own. She actually made her "rewarding" reaction possible by helping the infant organize his behavior in the first place.

Obviously, the caregiver is learning a great deal from this interactive play as well. The caregiver gets immediate feedback from the infant concerning the appropriateness of his or her efforts to build or lower the tension. The sensitive caregiver learns quickly to read the lookaways, smiles, puckers, and changes in muscular tension and, with experience, learns to anticipate the infant as well. One learns either to let the infant break contact or to de-escalate when signs appear suggesting the tension is too great. As you can learn to respond appropriately to your baby and to allow your baby space, you also can become skilled at what may be called *mood setting*. You ease the baby into play or into one activity from another; you do not thrust a playful interaction onto an otherwise occupied young infant. Through mood setting you actually establish the climate in which the appropriate degree of tension can be developed and organized reactions to you can occur. Then you can respond to them.

Thus, the sensitive caregiver is involved at a variety of levels in the interaction: setting it up, guiding it, maintaining a rich and varied context, and responding to the infant. It seems like a very complex task for you, indeed. But your infant will teach you every aspect of the process.

Play and Attachment

In my mind, the most important outcome of playful interaction during infancy is what occurs between the infant and caregiver; that its consequences for their relationship. The shorthand term for this process is *attachment,* which was introduced in Chapter 5. Studies of both humans and other primates suggest that attachment—the closeness, familiarity, and security in the bond with another— originally derives from close physical contact. In Harlow's famous studies, Rhesus monkeys derived some security from a soft, hugable, cloth model rather than from a model made of wire, even though food was received from the wire "mother." When frightened, these young monkeys could gain some security by clinging to the cloth mother, but they would not go to the wire "mother" that had "fed" them and could not use that model as a base for exploration. Physical contact is an important basis for attachment and security.

Playful interaction is of vital importance, because it allows the infant to make the transition from the physical holding base of attachment to a psychological holding. The caregiver holds the infant with eyes and voice, and the infant learns to be secure within this intimacy. The long, loving looks between caregiver and infant, punctuated by smiles that release tension and communicate pleasure, cement this bond.

To be sure, physical contact remains important, but early caregiver–infant play has a basic role in promoting the transition to an internalized attachment, to a feeling of security based on the *knowledge* that the caregiver is available and cares, and to an affective *sharing* between caregiver and infant. Each of you can express your feelings across a distance. An increasing flexibility to engage novel aspects of the environment results as the infant can derive a sense of security from progressively more distal cues. There is much greater freedom to explore and learn when the infant can range away

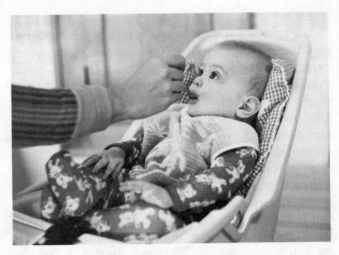

Figure 6-3. The spoon-feeding situation is an opportunity for intimacy and for play. (Photo: Hunt Greene.)

from the mother than when he or she must be sitting on her lap.

From being physically held, to face-to-face contact, to the glance across the room, the infant makes strides toward feelings of security and closeness even when distant. Increasingly, the feelings of security become internalized. Ultimately, the knowledge that he or she is loved will be sufficient. Ultimately, so will the knowledge that he or she is lovable. Face-to-face play, as the first step from the base of physical holding, is of fundamental importance.

The Infant's Own Play

In interactive play with your infant, both of you learn. You learn to be responsive to your baby in keeping with its particular nature and particular signal system. The infant learns a great deal in terms of self-control, tension tolerance, and reciprocal interaction. The infant also learns to organize responses, to coordinate schemes, and, in general, develops a sense of what Michael Lewis has called "generalized expectancy" and others have called effectance or competence.

These crucial developments, which are discussed below, also have important ties to play with siblings and solitary play. It is important for you to know that as crucial as your interactive play is, your baby also *needs* to have time for solitary play. Being responsive to your infant's signals is not the same thing as attempting to solve all problems for your baby. He or she can learn a great deal from siblings and from solitary play. Brazelton has pointed out in his book, *Infants and mothers,* that infants learn by trial and error, by repetition, by laboriously struggling to outcomes *by themselves.* At times it will be important for you to let your infant strive toward mastery independently, even though he or she will experience some frustrations and failures in the process. Very important learning results. If you are too easily hooked into solving all problems for the infant, it becomes more interested in drawing you in than in the results of its own actions.

Perhaps the mortar of cognitive development is the learning of connections, connections between sights and sounds or other sensory impressions, connections between actions and results, connections between the infant's action and your action. Coordination of schemes and the sense of effectance (competence, generalized expectancy) both refer to such associations or correlations in experience. When the infant learns to correlate (put together) his sensorimotor knowledge of you as a visual experience and you as touchable, with the sound **89**

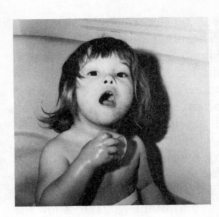

Figure 6-4. Any situation is an opportunity for play. (Photo: G. Sroufe.)

of your voice, your smell, and your manner of behaving, a concept of *you* as a person emerges. You are the seeable, touchable. . . . You well may be the first object that is more than the sum of separate impressions. Through the coordination of impressions, in large part by way of playful interaction, you become an integrated concept for the baby. You become mother or father or caregiver. Ultimately, the awareness that these coordinated impressions derive from its actions with respect to you leads the infant to a sense of the self, of himself or herself as a person.[1]

Likewise, when the infant has repeated experience with an action leading to a result, he begins to sense the connection between the two. Your play is important in this in that you can respond reliably to the infant's action. But objects respond reliably, too. When the infant shakes a rattle, it rattles every time. When she or he pushes on the stroller, it moves. When the cup is dropped, it falls with a crash. As development proceeds, the infant goes beyond these specific experiences to the general sense that actions have results, that

90   [1] I am indebted to my former student, Everett Waters, for these ideas.

he or *she* can make results occur. Your play with the infant is important here; but for generalized expectancy, for a general belief in its ability to have an effect, the infant also needs a wide variety of experience with the object world.

At the same time that the infant is developing a sense of competence or effectance, it also is learning about the limitations of its power and about physical law. Physical law cannot be violated; it is highly reliable. If the infant leans so that his center of gravity is not over his feet, he will fall. If he pushes his cup over the edge of the highchair tray, it will drop to the floor. An inanimate object will not move to the infant, however much he wants it.

Such frustrating confrontations with reality, such lessons in the limitations of actions, play a crucial role in development. I am, of course, not advocating deliberately frustrating your infant or forcing a precocious self-reliance. When your three-month-old drops a rattle, you naturally would retrieve it, unless, of course, other activities were more pressing. You would not have frustrating the child as a goal. When your ten-month-old drops something, however, much is to be gained by letting him solve the problem by himself when this is possible. The child analyst Erik Erikson has assured us that *children do not become neurotic because of frustration. Frustration is a part of life. They become neurotic only when the frustration is capricious and arbitrary, without meaning.* You cannot protect your child from all frustration, and it is not so terrible that you cannot.

Letting your child solve his own problems— getting unstuck when he has crawled into a tight spot, getting down from the couch, retrieving the toy, and so on—does more than define the limits **91** of his abilities. It helps expand his competence. As Piaget has said, both accommodation and assimilation are vital parts of the learning process. Assimilation, you recall, is the tendency of the infant to repeat the same action over and over (looking, mouthing, and so on), perhaps on a variety of objects. Such exercise is important. But encounters with failures of assimilation are also vital. When it won't fit or "won't go," the action must be modified to incorporate the new situation. It is in this way that actions (schemes) become differentiated and broadened. When the infant cannot reach the toy, he may pull the cloth it is on to get it and have an early encounter with tool-using. With repetitions of such an experience, he may get the *idea* of using objects in the environment as means to achieving goals.

Especially during the second half of the first year, your infant will become very skilled at using you to achieve ends. He will cry for you when he cannot get something, and he may even get in jams because he has learned this will bring you to him. All of this is an important part of his developing sense of effectance. You want him to learn people can be counted on. You want him to learn that you will respond to him as well as make demands. But you also want him to learn to trust in his own competence, and you want him to acquire capacities appropriate to his developmental level. You must coordinate both being a source of support and letting your infant do what he or she can do. One help in achieving this balance is sometimes to let your infant try to solve the problem before you step in. Another help is to watch your infant unobserved. You may be amazed at its resourcefulness. Brazelton argues convincingly that you also will discover that the infant experiences great joy in its own problem solving, in its own accomplishments.

Summary

For the infant, play *is* learning and learning *is* play. Infants learn through action. There is an inherent reward in doing, witnessed by the obvious involvement and pleasure of infants as they repeat newly discovered actions over and over. Both interactive play with caregivers (and siblings) and solitary play are of great importance in the infant's development. With you, important social learning occurs. A sense of the self, a sense of the trustworthiness of others, and a sense of mutual participation are acquired. But for the general sense of competence or effectance, solitary play, with its rewarding and frustrating aspects, is also fundamental. Self-solution (discovery for yourself) and discovery of self are tied together. The job of the caregiver involves capitalizing on the infant's built-in joy in doing and learning, guiding personal and interpersonal development, and providing the backdrop and basic experience for learning about the world. It also involves leaving the infant space, space to participate in the interaction, and space for doing and learning by herself or himself.

Sources

BRAZELTON, T. B. *Infants and mothers.* New York: Delacorte Press, 1969.

BRAZELTON, T. B., KOSLOWSKI, B., & MAIN, M. The origins of reciprocity: The early mother–infant interaction. **93**

In M. Lewis & L. Rosenblum (Eds.), *The effect
of the infant on its caregiver.* New York: John
Wiley and Sons, Inc., © 1974.

BREGER, L. *From instinct to identity: The development
of personality.* Englewood Cliffs, N.J.: Prentice-
Hall, Inc., 1974.

ERIKSON, E. *Childhood and society.* New York: Norton
& Co., 1950.

HARLOW, H., & ZIMMERMANN, R. Affectional responses
in the infant monkey. *Science,* 1959, *130,* 421–32.

LEWIS, M., & GOLDBERG, S. Perceptual–cognitive development in infancy: A generalized expectancy
model as a function of the mother–infant interaction. *Merrill-Palmer Quarterly,* 1969, *15,* 81–100.

PIAGET, J., & INHELDER, B. *The psychology of the child.*
New York: Basic Books, 1969.

SROUFE, L. A., & MITCHELL, P. Emotional development.
In J. Osofsky (Ed.), *Handbook of infant development.* New York: John Wiley and Sons, Inc.,
in press.

STERN, D. The goal and structure of mother–infant play.
*Journal of the American Academy of Child
Psychiatry,* 1974, *13,* 402–21.

WHITE, R. Motivation reconsidered: The concept of
competence. *Psychological Review,* 1959, *66,*
297–333.

AN OUTLINE
OF DEVELOPMENT

7

An Overview of Development in the First Year

This is the nature of development. Skills and capacities that were fleeting and irregular, almost chance occurrences, become reliable and more completely under control of the infant.

You now have some idea of the nature of situations producing smiling and laughter in infants as they develop. By noting what causes the baby to smile or laugh at different ages you have acquired some sense of the time course of development in the first year of life. In understanding the relationships among smiling, laughter, and fear and among affective expression, play, and cognitive (mental) development, you also have acquired some idea of the nature of development.

Development is an integrated, organized process. The developing child is viewed as a changing system, so that different phases of development (affective, social, cognitive) are seen to go forward in an interlocking, coordinated manner. Cognitive development influences affective expression; for example, the development of memory enables the **97** infant to laugh in anticipation of mother's re-appearance from behind a cloth and to show fear when confronting a previously experienced negative situation within an insecure context. Likewise, changing affective expression influences cognitive and social development, as when early smiles of recognition attract caregivers to more active involvement with the infant.

To develop this perspective further, it is necessary to present a more detailed picture of development in the first year. An outline of the most significant acquisitions, month by month, is presented, though it is assumed that by now you know that ages given are only approximate. Then there is a description of some of the major themes of development as they unfold across the first year. This is a prelude to a final integration of general developmental trends in the first year with the unfolding of emotions, followed by a discussion of development in the second year of life (Chapter 9).

In following the description of growth in the first year, three models of developmental process may be useful. The one that has my primary allegiance is outlined in Chapter 2. Following Dr. René Spitz and others, this model emphasizes converging lines of development and sees growth as a series of reorganizations. This conception is consistent with the idea presented in the last chapter of a critical mass of experience, with subcapacities being prerequisite for the emergence of an integrated skill. The idea is that with sufficient opportunities to experience and to act within one way of operating on the world, with sufficient variety of exposure within this way of operating, and with complementary maturation, new ways of engaging the environment emerge. At first all sensations are treated as equivalent, but later the infant distinguishes between those coming from within and those coming from the external world. And after repeatedly exercising its separate capacities to see, hear, and touch the caregiver and so forth, the infant develops the capacity to respond to the caregiver (or to an object) as an integrated entity. This again is a qualitative turn in development, paving the way for truly mutual, interpersonal interaction and further developing the sense of the self. The caregiver now can exist when absent, can be anticipated, and can be called for.

Another model of development is more closely associated with T. G. R. Bower, a Scottish psychologist. He stresses the idea that infants are highly competent at every age, even in the newborn period. In fact, competencies that exist at one stage of development are sometimes lost and must be reacquired in a new way. For example, when language emerges and becomes the infant's primary form of conceptualizing, many properties of the object world known in a sensorimotor manner apparently are lost. This is because the child seeks to apply its linguistic abilities, though at first they are poorly developed. The concepts will be reacquired, of course, and—it may be argued—in a more sophisticated, deeper way. Another example is the walking reflex. If you support your very young infant in the standing position, it will make alternating, walking movements of its legs. Later, along with other reflexes of the newborn period, this reflex will drop out. In the case of walking, it appears as a skill late in the first year or early in the second year.

Another model, which could be related to Bower's, emphasizes what might be termed *emotional regressions*. This idea, which is consistent with some psychoanalytic thinking, also has been described by Brazelton in his book, *Infants and mothers.* It implies that prior to new, important developmental achievements, there may be periods of renewed dependency and fearfulness. Just prior to walking, for example, infants may show regressed motor behavior and a period of renewed physical clinging to the caregiver.

The validity of each of these models will be apparent in the following outline of development. Rather than being in competition, together they describe the complex nature of development. All are in agreement that development is not best conceptualized as a steady, incremental process. It goes forward with leaps and bounds and periods of consolidation and stepping back as well. New skills are not simply added on top of old ones. They sometimes replace old skills and sometimes incorporate them in hierarchical or integrated fashion; that is, the old skills become part of a more complex action. At many or perhaps all points in development it makes sense to think of the infant as transformed, as a qualitatively different being (whose understanding of the world is closer to that of the adult than an infant of an earlier period).

The outline and synthesis of development that follow in this chapter and the next two have been drawn primarily from a developmental psychology textbook by T. G. R. Bower, from Brazelton's *Infants and mothers,* an old but exceptionally interesting book by Charlotte Bühler *(The first year of life),* the writings of René Spitz and Robert Emde and their associates, and my own observations, research, and papers on emotional development. Were I to recommend one book for infant caregivers it would be Brazelton's, because of its completeness, readability, and accuracy. It contains a wealth of information about almost every aspect of the infant's physical development and emotional needs.

In the Beginning

In many ways the newborn comes remarkably well equipped for the adaptation it must make (Figure 7-1). One of its notable coping mechanisms is its capacity to deal with noxious or traumatic experiences. Following traumatic experiences (for example, circumcision), infants sleep a profoundly deep sleep (a total refractory period) that allows physical and psychological recovery. Likewise, newborns startle and cry in response to a single strong stimulus (e.g., loud sound), but remarkably, their reactions diminish in response to subsequent intense stimulation. Ultimately, they may even go to sleep if the stimulation is continued. Such protective reactions are vital for the labile, vulnerable newborn.

According to T. G. R. Bower, infants have a great many other competencies in the first weeks of life, as well. To witness these competencies, one must make certain that the infant is in a receptive, alert state, and free to exhibit existing motor skills. Bower argues that young infants are not often in a state to demonstrate their competencies but that the competencies exist if one seeks them carefully. (There is rapid development of changes in dominant state.)

As we said in our review of smiling, infants certainly have considerable capacity for attending to and sensing their environment, at least under ideal conditions. They smile at voices, they follow slowly moving objects with their eyes, they will at

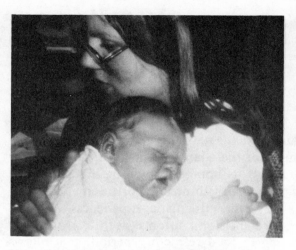

Figure 7-1. The newborn comes well equipped for the adaptation it must make. Here a newborn molds to the caregiver. (Photo: T. Baxter.)

times look in the direction of sounds, and they actually have quite good visual acuity. They certainly are well equipped for taking in information. According to Bower, they also make some basic responses to physical objects; for example, they are more likely to reach toward an object if it is near than if it is far; they blink or show a defensive response to an object approaching the face; they become upset if they reach for an "apparent object," created by an optical illusion, that is not really there. Again, such capacities would occur only under ideal conditions; for example, the defensive reaction to the approaching object would be observed only when the baby was alert and was propped up into a sitting position with pillows, and only when the object moved slowly enough that the infant could follow it.

Though further research may show that Bower and others who stress early competence are correct in many instances, it is still clear that cortical (higher brain) development is extremely limited in the early weeks. The *reflexive* nature of early behavior shows in qualitative comparisons with later skills. For example, early blinking is *in reaction* to the apparently approaching object; later responses may occur in anticipation of the "collision" and may include blocking the object with the hands or turning away.[1] Early reaching has an uncoordinated, random character. When the baby is attending a near-in object, the hands move in its direction as part of a general "turning toward," an orienting of the whole organism toward the object. Later, reaching is precise and coordinated; the infant sees the object, reaches directly for it, and grasps it. Similarly, Burton White describes the *automatic* character of early visual behavior. The infant will track the same object with its eyes over and over as long as it is physically able. The object elicits the visual following. Later, it is *the infant* that looks at the object, and it may follow it only once or not at all if it is not of interest.

The Second and Third Months

Many observers agree that there is a qualitative turning point in development at the second or third month. However competent the newborn may be, a dramatic increase in competence is observed at this time. Among other things, there is a great increase in attention to the external environment and receptivity to stimulation. The infant is awake more and alert more, spends much less time fussing, and as a consequence, it is visually attentive to the things around it (Figure 7-2). It can hold its

---

[1]Observation of my students, Dante Cicchetti and Linda Mans.   **103**

head up with ease and can sustain postures so that there can be continuity in its visual experiences. The infant now will interrupt feeding to open its eyes, and eye-to-eye contact with the caregiver becomes increasingly long. Tension tolerance is increased markedly. The baby is no longer so easily upset by stimulation and so avoids strident stimulation less. It now can begin to coordinate two sense organs with relative ease—for example, seeking the source of a sound. It pays attention to its own movements and vocalizations and those of others. In brief, in Charlotte Bühler's words, the infant now "subjects itself" to the stimulation, with engagement becoming more continuous. Increased social responsivity and rapid development in all spheres follow from this new receptivity to the environment.

Figure 7-2. Motor development, increasing periods of being awake and alert, and a psychological "turning toward" are coordinated to support the 3-month-old's engagement of its world. (Photo: E. Bushnell.)

As a derivation of this increased receptivity to external experience, the infant learns, for example, to bring its hands (or feet) to its mouth with ease.

As Brazelton states, in this behavior the infant learns about the gratifying stimulation at both ends, laying the groundwork for a coordination of vision, touch, and mouthing. After a fashion it can grasp a dangling object successfully—for example, a rattle hanging in the crib. Moreover, for the first time, it learns to coordinate its action with an outcome. Research has shown that it can learn to turn its head in complex combinations (e.g., Right Right Left Left) in order to turn on a light. You can observe your baby learn to shake the rattle with its hand (or more easily by kicking its feet) *to produce* the sound. Such "awareness" must be primitive to be sure, but like the smiles of recognition (Chapter 3) it is a beginning toward a true sense of mastery of the surroundings.

The Fourth Month

Brazelton has provided a very informative description of the three-month-old (the fourth month) at play with himself:

> Louis played for as much as three-quarters of an hour at a time on his back. He watched his hands, brought them up together, played with his fingers, and took an interest in each hand in front of him. He would look back and forth from one hand to the other, bring them together, smiling as he did so, and grinned as he grabbed one with the other. He would hold on to each hand, pull his arms apart, and fairly snap them away from each other. He giggled as they snapped (p. 118).
>
> He reached repeatedly for toys on his cradle gym, grabbing hold of one, pulling it toward him, and letting it bounce away as he let go. He seemed to be able to do this with each hand, and, by the end of the fourth month, took some pleasure in alternating hands to grab the objects. It seemed to his mother as if he were making a distinction between one hand and the other (p. 119).

In this play the four-month-old is learning to differentiate the parts of his body, just as in the social realm he is learning to differentiate known from unknown persons. At this time his smile is captured more readily by his caregivers and other family members than by unfamiliar persons. In the wake of the increased alertness and attentiveness of the third month, in the fourth month the infant has become notably more sensitive to the caregiver's mood. Even younger babies react to tenseness or anxiety of their caregivers, but this will be more apparent to you in the fourth month.

Noteworthy advances are made in the intellectual sphere as well, especially with regard to the coordination of schemes—the integration of perceptions and/or actions with other perceptions and/or actions. Whereas the two-month-old could look consistently to the source of a sound, the three-month-old can gaze at its hand while touching an object and use its hand to explore properties of the object (rubbing it, squeezing it). Such concurrent experiences with touch and vision and with watching the act of touching lead the three-month-old to construct a much more coordinated and integrated world than that of the two-month-old. In this month or the next, the infant will continue looking with some consistency in the direction an object was moving. This reflects motoric roots of what later will be the sense of object permanence (see seventh and eighth months).

The Fifth Month

Though such a comment also could be made at earlier points, you may notice that the fifth month (age four months) is characterized by a rapid expansion of motor skills and a new energy in approaching the environment. By this time the infant's interest in the surroundings is such that feeding will be punctuated with periods of surveying the scene, smiling at the caregiver, and so forth. Infants can sit well in infant seats (and even tip them over), and such posturing leaves them freer to use their hands.

Perhaps the major achievement of the fifth month is the relatively complete mastery of hand-eye and hand-to-mouth coordination. By the end of the fifth month, the infant can reach and grasp with a sureness and directness any object within range, adjusting the hand to fit the object (Figure 7-3). With facility, it can transfer toys from either hand to the mouth and from one hand to the other, which enables changing tactile as well as visual perspective. This facility with coordinating schemes promotes a rapid expansion of knowledge about objects.

Also in the fifth month, the roots of two developmental processes of great importance become apparent. One of these is "intentionality." By this time certain coordinated actions are so well mastered (e.g., seeing and grasping, grasping and mouthing), that if part of the action is initiated the infant is motivated to exercise the complete action. The infant will cry when it cannot reach an object it sees or can reach it but is not able to pull it to the mouth. Brazelton describes an example of the latter situation:

> The force behind this integration can be aroused in a baby of this age by leaving him with a toy that he cannot pull into him. He is left with vision and fingers. He will play happily this way for a period. Then, as if he suddenly realizes this is not enough, his frustration builds up as he strains to get his mouth on it. He ends up by screaming furiously when he cannot examine it all over with his mouth and hands, as well as his eyes (p. 131).

107

Figure 7-3. Visually directed reaching is well mastered by the 5-month-old. Note the anticipatory hand posturing. (Photo: G. & W. Piccolo.)

This is the very beginning of truly purposeful, goal-oriented behavior. Such purposefulness is also seen when the four- or five-month-old vocalizes to get the caregiver's attention or interrupts conversations.

The second crucial developmental process becoming apparent in the fifth month is imitation. I do not consider true imitation to emerge until later, but at this time the caregiver can get the infant to repeat sounds already made. The infant makes the sound. The caregiver repeats it, and in response to this repetition the infant makes the sound again. Later the infant will imitate behaviors it was not performing at the time and even those it has never done before.

The Sixth Month

Trends begun in the fifth month are continued here. Ever more active, many babies now have some means of locomotion, perhaps rolling over from one place to another, scooting on their stomachs, or utilizing some combination of movements. Characteristically, the parts of the movement act are practiced to mastery and then pieced together. The activity clearly is more coordinated, more polished, and better organized than in the fifth month. Delight in motor achievements also is becoming more apparent, as in the infant's squeals of delight as he or she stands with the help of the bounce seat.

Intentionality and the sense of object permanence advance. By this time infants are quite likely to cry if an intended movement or posture fails. Budding intentionality also is shown when crying is produced by an adult entering but not approaching the infant. By this age many infants also will drop toys from the highchair and scream for their return and in some way may "call for" the caregiver when he or she is in another room. Perhaps in other ways as well one will see the dawning of object permanence (the idea that objects and persons continue to exist even when they cannot be sensed directly by the infant); for example, the infant may show "positive surprise" (Bühler) when an object that has been taken away is returned.

The Seventh Month

As is the nature of growth, motor development, which has already been rapid, now explodes. Many infants now creep (scoot) with facility, though many others, of course, will not for a while yet. The new freedom to creep makes them more aware of the caregiver's whereabouts, and infants are now more likely to call or cry for caregivers when they are not present, especially when a toy is inaccessible or when they get themselves stuck. Similarly, the new ability to sit unassisted, freeing the hands for exploration, has profound implications for the development of skill with and knowledge about the object world.

Earlier the hand was an extension of the self. Now objects may be used as an extension of the hand. One object may be used to poke at or push another, or two objects may be banged together. While in a sitting position, an object may be passed back and forth from hand to hand. As extensions of the infant, objects acquire greater importance; now an infant is likely to cry if an object is pushed to an inaccessible place. In part because of the pursuit of "lost" objects, the infant increases its interpersonal effectance—namely, the ability to call on the caregivers for assistance.

In addition to the developing sense of object permanence, there may be other evidence of emerging memory capacity at this time. According to Brazelton, infants now show that they expect father (or mother) to enter when the front door opens at the end of the day, that they know food is coming when they hear the refrigerator door open, and show disappointment (or fear) when the elderly lady turns out not to be grandmother. They also may be shy of the sofa after falling in an attempt to pull to a stand by themselves.

By this age, infants are babbling and cooing a great deal and may do so deliberately to gain attention. Vocal imitation is emerging, as is vocal "dialogue" between caregiver and infant, though of course the roots of reciprocity (mutual give and take) were seen even earlier.

The Eighth Month

Increasingly, it becomes more difficult to specify the exact age at which various developmental milestones are achieved, and again there is no evidence that somewhat earlier or later achievement has any implications for later intellectual ability. Except in extreme cases, early performance on developmental tests does not predict performance on infant tests given later or on preschool intelligence tests. Only after about age two are such test scores very predictive.

Still, in the eighth month (age seven months) or ninth month, most babies will crawl with some skill, though others will not crawl until later. Generally, motor development continues to unfold rapidly. Many babies will by this time pull themselves to a stand and edge along the furniture. Such standing usually precedes skill at crawling. The pincer grasp (thumb and forefinger juxtaposed) is commonly available, and a finer manipulation of objects is therefore possible.

If I had to say a specific age, it is during the eighth or ninth month that object permanence has arrived in a clear way. In our studies[2] we used a trick tray on a highchair, such that we could drop the toy through a trap door after covering it with our hands. It was in the eighth or ninth month that infants tried to move our hands, showed surprise or interest when the toy was gone, and actively searched for it by opening our hands or looking on the floor. They also looked to our faces, as if to say, "What have you done?" and then looked back again to the empty tray. I remember one

---

[2]Research conducted with William Charlesworth.

eight-month-old who pounded a "What's going on here?" on the tray with his fist after his search failed to turn up the toy. Other evidence of an emerging sense of object permanence is anticipation of your return or anticipating the crash of an object dropped to the floor. The infant knows that you and the object continue to exist and act even when not in view.

The relationship of general developmental trends to emotional development is the topic of the next chapter, but it should be mentioned here that this is the age at which one commonly sees the beginnings of stranger fear and separation protest, though sober faces for strangers appeared earlier. It is also the age at which our study indicated an explosion in social laughter, laughter to games and to peekaboo in particular (with the baby even pulling the cover off your face if you wait too long). Laughter in anticipation of your "return" in peekaboo is, of course, a reflection of the sense of object permanence.

The Ninth Month

The business of putting parts of motor behaviors into complex wholes continues. By this time many babies can put together the well-practiced skills required to get from their stomachs to a standing position, and they are highly motivated to do so.

Object permanence and competence with objects become more solid; for example, infants now will engage in long searches for hidden objects and will not be distracted by other objects. Objects can be handled with great precision, and one block may be stacked on top of another, illustrating both a growth of muscular coordination and the rudiments of a constructive "plan." The infant also now may crawl and gather several objects, bringing them together.

Rapid cognitive growth is apparent in the social sphere as well. By the end of the ninth month, the infant may be quite capable of imitating behaviors he or she never has done before. Even deferred imitation may appear; that is, the infant may imitate an action seen a short time or even a day before. Likewise, a more sophisticated participation in social games may emerge. The infant may bring the ball to you and clearly show anticipation of its part in the interchange.

Stranger fear and separation protest may become more apparent. "Transitional" objects may make their appearance—a special blanket, another soft object, or even a toy that the infant seems to need present at all times as a source of security. Brazelton has suggested that such periods of fearfulness (periods of increased dependency) may be the precursors of new spurts of independence.

The Tenth Month

Strides are seen in motor skill, understanding of and skill with objects, intentionality, and social participation. At this age, if not somewhat earlier or later, you may see your infant walking with the help of furniture or his infant seat, grinning from ear to ear as he shoves the support along. The infant now differentiates the hands, using one primarily for carrying, the other for securing and manipulating objects. The ability to transport objects while continuing to explore new ones opens up new possibilities for comparison. One advance **113** toward using objects as tools, which may appear at this age, is throwing one object at a second unreachable object, a further extension of the self through use of the environment.

An expanded and more serviceable memory capacity and perceptivity is seen in social situations. The infant may try to get you or a sibling to return to a game from the day before. The infant becomes a more *active participant* in social games, perhaps initiating hiding games, crawling from you to be chased, and continuing games that you start. One capacity that Brazelton describes at this age is a quickness to perceive in the social situation. When a mother laughed when her infant flopped on his face while crawling across the room, the infant began to do it on purpose, and soon they were laughing together.

Separation problems and stranger fear still may be building, reaching their peak even later in the first year, but the infant becomes more active in coping with these problems. At the same time his or her sensitivity to moods and affective expression by the caregiver is increasing. You also may see the beginnings of acted crying, feigned distress to produce a result.

By the End: The Eleventh and Twelfth Months

The infant's competence by the end of the first year is truly amazing (Figure 7-4). Many are walking joyfully with assistance and some without aid, although crawling is typically still the mode for serious mobility. They are intrepid explorers, systematically "casing" a new room and checking out each toy. Objects can be used in combination, will be sought when lost, and even can be "fetched" when requested by the caregiver. Memory is remarkable. Tool-using is expanding; for example, the infant can use a string to pull a toy within reach. Primitive language now is being used with some consistency for making desires known.

Figure 7-4. The infant exercises its achievements with increasing delight. (Photo: P. LaSota.)

In general, capacities that you have glimpsed earlier are now quite clear. For example, there is no question about object permanence. The baby even remembers where things are from some time earlier. Its skill in manipulating and combining is equally impressive. Many things you thought your baby could do earlier you now see it performing much more adequately. Both of your perceptions are correct. This is the nature of development. Skills and capacities that were fleeting and irregular, almost chance occurrences, become reliable and more completely under control of the infant.

It is at the end of the first year that Jerome Kagan finds evidence for hypothesis generation. Infants know enough about the world that they ex- **115** pect certain outcomes and certain cause–effect relationships. They have become more active causal agents. It is now also that our work has shown them to be incredibly sensitive to situation, sequence of events, and other aspects of context; the infant acts in response to past experience and anticipated outcome as well as to present influences.

Socially, the year-old is quite mature. When frightened, he or she may seek your glance as if to say, "Did you see that?" Also, the infant is now much more likely to play the joke on you, putting something in your mouth and laughing, covering your face, or hiding a toy from a sibling and laughing when it is found. Virtually any action or speech sound can be imitated, even behaviors you did not intend to be imitated! So complete is the infant's imitative skill that he or she can imitate actions that cannot be seen (sticking out the tongue), can imitate actions done the day before (deferred imitation), and can make new applications of acts through imitation—that is, imitate the act in a different but appropriate situation.

Sources

BOWER, T. G. R. *Development in infancy.* San Francisco: W. H. Freeman and Co., 1974.

BRAZELTON, T. B. *Infants and mothers.* New York: Delacourt Press, 1969.

BÜHLER, C. *The first year of life.* New York: The John Day Co., 1920.

EMDE, R., GAENSBAUER, T., & HARMON, R. Emotional expression in infancy: A biobehavioral study. *Psychological Issues Monograph Series,* 1976.

S<small>ROUFE</small>, L. A. The ontogenesis of the emotions. In J. Osofsky (Ed.), *Handbook of infant development*. New York: John Wiley and Sons, Inc., in press.

S<small>ROUFE</small>, L. A., & M<small>ITCHELL</small>, P. Emotional development. In J. Osofsky (Ed.), *Handbook of infant development*. New York: John Wiley and Sons, Inc., in press.

S<small>ROUFE</small>, L. A., W<small>ATERS</small>, E., & M<small>ATAS</small>, L. Contextual determinants of infant affective response. In M. Lewis & L. Rosenblum (Eds.), *The origins of fear*. New York: John Wiley and Sons, Inc., 1974.

8

The Beginnings of Emotions

Not only do emotions closely reflect the infant's cognitive development, they are, in a way, the meaning system around which all early development is organized. All engagement of the environment is marked by interest or wariness, attack or retreat, embracing or withdrawal. And the unfolding of the emotions shows the increasingly complex and differentiated reactions of the developing infant. Whereas cognitive performance reflects the developing mental capacity of the child, the expression of emotion reveals the developing child as a person.

An outline of development, month by month, can be instructive, and it certainly makes baby watching more interesting. But in ways it is somewhat artificial. Development does not occur on a monthly basis. It occurs in terms of unfolding, progressive sequences, with *order* the dominant theme rather than rigid timing. Nor do the sequential developments in various domains occur in isolation. They are interlocking, mutually influencing, and they occur against the backdrop of important, general developmental tendencies. (Recall the biological model presented in Chapter 2.)

General Characteristics of Development in the First Year

In this chapter I sketch some of the more general characteristics of development in the first year, trace some of the critical themes in terms of their stages rather than ages, and finally, attempt to weave these themes together into a coherent pattern with implications for emotional development.

From Uncoordinated to Purposeful Action

An examination of developmental changes in what can be called *motoric reactions* reveals a fundamental characteristic of development. In the beginning the newborn is characterized by uncoordinated, purposeless, unrepeatable movements. The awake infant is in constant motion, but the movements are basically random and unrelated to external events. This continual movement represents what Charlotte Bühler has called "the pressing activity with which the living being is born." Soon, however, a progression begins toward purposeful acts of mastery and creation.

The very first acts may be characterized as "impulsive," what might be called "single movements," and are not repeated, not purposeful, and not organized with other movements into a precise act. There is, of course, some coordination of behavior even quite early. As discussed earlier, if the infant's eyes are fixed on an object, especially at the midline (directly in front of it), excitation may build and the subsequent movements are "directed" at the object. But these are really not volitional movements in the true sense. If it bumps **119** the object it does not appear any more likely to do so again than it was in the first place.

It is when one sees the emergence of movements characterized by *care and foresight* (as when the infant looks at, then reaches for something), and the act is repeatable, that one can begin to speak of purposive behavior. The tendency to repeat simple acts and to enjoy such repetition has been referred to by the Bühlers and Piaget as "functional pleasure."

When one next sees persistence in action (with respect to an object, for example) and coordination and combination of separate movements into an act (sitting up, bringing two objects into contact, and so on), one legitimately may begin speaking of goals and intentions. It is in the successful pursuit of goals that one often encounters the "joy of mastery." As Bühler has stated, before the infant *enjoys* a specific *succession* of movements, he gives himself over to and finds *pleasure* in individual "bodily movements and vocalizations which become always more organized and rhythmic." *Joy* is "outwardly," "objectively" directed.

The progression toward more organized, coordinated activity advances so rapidly that by the end of the first year infants can carry out a complex series of acts (bring several toys together from various places) and exhibit elementary combinational and tool-using skills. They can stack blocks, knock one toy with another, and pull a toy in with a string.

What I have been describing is the general developmental tendency toward specification, precision, and coordination. What begins as random movement ends as directed, organized behavior by the second half of the first year. Buhler provides

a very instructive example of this specification

process with respect to negative reactions. Consider the infant having its nose cleaned. In this situation the newborn baby makes random, diffuse movements of all parts of the body, and these are *in reaction to* the swab contacting the nose. By one month, the child will turn the head aside in response to the cleaning, with arms and legs still flailing. Somewhat later the total body will engage in this flight response. But not until early in the second quarter is there a defensive reaction, a throwing back of the head and an arching of the body. This is still an uncoordinated, impulsive reaction, "going off in all directions," but it may accidentally be successful in hindering the cleaning (blocking the stimulus), as when the infant's hand gets in the way of the caregiver. "In the fifth month the defense movement . . . becomes a real pushing away, and a sixth month child deters the action by firmly holding the hand of the grown up" (p. 22).

Later the defense will occur as soon as the object approaches, and finally it will occur even when the particular object never has caused harm. As we shall see, what begins as diffuse negative reactions becomes fear and anger by the second half-year of life.

There is an interesting difference in the development of negative reactions compared to positive reactions. Passive positive reactions (simple smiles) precede active outbreaks of joy, whereas vigorous motoric expressions of negative affect precede passing negative expressions. Active joy becomes prominent in the third quarter-year, and early in the second half-year one also observes for the first time quiet crying with the body still (Bühler). By twelve months, the negative affect may no longer be a *reaction* to a particular noxious event but is a more general feeling or mood. It seems reasonable that early in life a full expression of negative affect is an important capability for the vulnerable infant. Also, in keeping with our ideas about tolerating and transforming tension and how these capacities develop, one would expect a parallel development of the ability to contain the negative reaction (to differentiate it away from an all-or-none experience) and the occurrence of vigorous positive affect.

The motoric components of fear and anger likewise proceed from global, diffuse reactions to quite specific and directed behaviors. For example, with fear reactions there is a trend from a general reaction to a part movement such as gaze aversion with the body remaining still. At first the infant remains locked into a captivating event until sufficient tension develops to produce total distress. Later it learns to avoid or glance away from the object, thus modulating the impact of the event. Of course, events also can frighten the older infant, but, as we shall discuss, this is because of negative meaning, not from a build-up of tension due to behavioral fixation. And the reaction can be quite varied.

From Passive Receptivity
to Active Interest

At the same time behavioral specification is taking place, an important developmental sequence in the infant's motivational structure unfolds. The newborn is rarely in a receptive state; it is either sleeping or experiencing the press of biological needs much of the time. It is characterized by relative passivity. But as you know, daytime sleep decreases rapidly, and before the first quarter-year of life ends the infant shows a clear readiness to reception—openness to stimulation from the surroundings—and a

reduced tendency to react aversively to stimulation.
It now pays attention to its own movements and
vocalizations and those of others, which makes
possible further development in all spheres. In the
next few months and throughout the remainder of
the first year, the infant moves from passive reception to "interest" and increasingly to active interest.
In the second half-year the child is seeking stimuli
actively and persistently, not just reacting to them
when encountered. It creates its own sensory stimulation and even creates new objects by combining
objects encountered. There is a stretching and
leaning toward objects of interest and, with mobility, approach movements of the whole body. By
the end of the first year the infant *can and will*
unleash a series of actions on an object, pursue an
object even in the face of distraction, retrieve it
when temporarily out of sight, return to it another
day, seek it when lost, and protest its loss if its
persistent efforts are unsuccessful. Such directedness
and persistence is what is meant by *active* interest.

Expanded and generalized interest becomes
curiosity and is the basis for systematic exploratory behavior seen by the end of the first year. It is
also the basis of positive surprise (surprise accom-
panied by recognition in a secure context) and
negative surprise, which is related to fear. The
active interest of the infant, the engagement with
the stimulation or object, produces a state of
dynamic tension and sets the stage for surprise
when the unexpected change occurs (see Chapter 5).
Surprise (Figure 8-1) is observed predominantly
in the second half of the first year when there is
both active interest and the cognitive capacities for
following transformations in stimulus situations
and processing rapid change (for example watching
Jack slowly disappear into the box, maintaining

Interest

Active Interest

Curiosity

Surprise

attention, and then processing the rapid reappearance).

Figure 8-1. Illustration of surprise expression. (Illustration: J. Roberts.)

Critical Themes in Development

With this consideration of general developmental characteristics as a background we can trace certain critical themes of development through the first year. These themes are not independent of general development, however; for example, motoric persistence and intentionality are closely related concepts. Likewise, the various themes are closely related to each other. Taken together, the general and more specific aspects of physical, cognitive, and social development make possible an understanding of the unfolding of the emotions.

Coordination of Schemes

Coordination of schemes is the simultaneous experience of two sensory impressions (for example, with regard to the body or an object), an action and a sensory experience, or two actions. One may
124 see and hear or touch and see an object, manipulate

an object and note it change visually, or call for mother and have her come. It is the relating of the two impressions and/or actions that is implied by the term *coordination*.

In a sense coordination of schemes has its roots in the first time the newborn infant smells the breast as it sucks or looks to the source of a sound. But clearly the period of receptivity at two to three months marks a crucial step. The infant can grasp, can put hand or foot in mouth, and has a vague sense of its actions having consequences. Soon after this period, he or she *watches* the hand while manipulating an object, reaches and grasps any object with skill, and puts anything to mouth. Next the infant begins simultaneously dealing with two objects at once, banging, rubbing, pushing. By the second half-year objects are seen, grasped, touched, mouthed, manipulated, acted on, and *used* to explore other objects. And so it progresses.

As emphasized in the chapter on play, making connections—that is, coordination of two or more aspects of experience—is vital for developing knowledge about objects. To manipulate something and to see it change visually while *at the same time* receiving the physical (tactile) sensations from your hand is to know the object much more than the simple sum of your visual and tactile experience. It is to know the object in a more whole way. Likewise, experiencing connections between your actions and changes in the environment is the basis for your feeling of potency or effectance. In a sense, it is the basis of all knowledge. Knowledge *is* the integration of experience.

Coordination of schemes is also the basis for laughter and fear. In fact, major theories of laughter and fear are explicitly founded on this notion. Anthony Ambrose, a British psychologist, has argued that laughter is an expression of ambiva-

Laughter

lence, expressing (i.e., coordinating) both positive and negative feelings or response tendencies concerning an event. Thus, he has argued that it would emerge in the fourth month when coordination of schemes becomes notable. We updated this view with our idea of tension in a secure context. The infant is able to experience the excitation or tension while at the same time experiencing the security of the context. Better put, because his experience of tension is within (coordinated with) his experience of security, the event can be coped with (integrated, assimilated, handled), and laughter results when relaxation follows the tension increase (see Chapter 4).

In the second half-year of life, the infant becomes sophisticated and precise in what it can coordinate, in part because of a greatly increased speed of processing information. It is at this time that the second type of laughter emerges. This is the laughter that is based not on physical jogging but on cognitive incongruity. The ability to see the twist in the event (mother sucking on bottle, behind a mask, with a dangling cloth in her mouth) is exactly the ability to coordinate schemes on a rather advanced level. For example, a memory of mother is coordinated with the visual image of the masked face. The ability to coordinate schemes is well launched before the middle of the first year and unfolds rapidly thereafter. Nonreflexive (cognitive) laughter follows suit, not coincidentally but because one and the same process is involved.

Fear, as opposed to startle or distress, also is seen at about the same time that laughter based on incongruity emerges. This makes sense. Fear is related to the ability and motivation to coordinate schemes. As was pointed out in Chapter 5, a prominent theory of fear or wariness is that it rep-

Fear

126

resents a failure of an experience to fit (be coordinated) with an expectation or model. The same type of incongruity can be involved as with nonreflexive laughter, but the incongruity cannot be resolved and occurs in an insecure context. Fear can also result, of course, when the infant has a renewed encounter with a previously noxious experience. Here, the present event is coordinated with the past experience.

Intentionality

Intentionality, the capacity and motivation to exercise an action or series of actions to achieve some end or goal, is central in many experiences of joy and in the unfolding of anger, the sense of naughtiness, and later in aggression and in the extension of the sense of naughtiness to actual feelings of guilt.

My position is that there is pleasure in a vaguely sensed production of an outcome but real joy when the outcome is intended and strived for. When an infant laboriously pushes to hands and **Joy** toes, raises itself to the standing position, gains its balance, and totters toward you on the couch, I am not surprised at the squeals of laughter. There is joy in mastery. The sustained engagement associated with an intended sequence of behavior produces tension or excitement (Chapter 5) and therefore, laughter.

Intentionality is also crucial in the emergence of anger. Very early the infant appears "mad" **Anger** when, for example, its head is restrained from movement or there is other restriction of its normal activities. This is a diffuse, flailing, negative reaction. Later, in the second quarter-year of life, it may cry when it cannot reach an object or bring **127** an object to its mouth. The progression toward a more clear directness of behavior continues, in parallel with the specification of motor behavior outlined earlier. And when behavioral tendencies are frustrated, negative affect results. Starting early in the second half-year, the infant's ability to direct a series of actions toward a goal and to persist in the attainment of the desired end unfolds rapidly.

An infant sees a ball. It crawls across the floor, largely ignoring other objects, and grabs for it. But the ball rolls under a chair. The infant reaches under the chair and even pushes on the chair but still cannot get the ball. It protests and cries in frustration.

Along with such goal orientation and persistence to achieve an end, the capacity to see the caregiver or other person as a block in the way of the goal develops at about this same time. When the infant has the degree of intentionality being described and the capacity to comprehend a person as blocking a goal, interpersonal anger will emerge. On the positive side such an expansion of coordination of schemes (seeing the caregiver as a means for achieving a goal) is also the root of interpersonal effectance—that is, the idea that people can be counted on for help in carrying out intentions. By late in the first year babies can cry on purpose. They learn this by becoming aware of the effects of crying.

In my view anger is an interpersonal affect, distinct from negative reactions to frustration in general.[1] Anger is expressed when the infant perceives you as interfering with its intended behavior.

---

[1] *Will* is a generalized intentionality that emerges in the first year and expands in the second. Brazelton has argued that the development of will is related to separation protest. You are leaving against the infant's will. Self-initiated separations are easier.

Seen in this way, anger is a perfectly normal emotion, as healthy as joy or fear. It emerges naturally as a *directed,* specific reaction to frustration, reflecting a rather advanced ability to recognize the source of the frustration. (Later in childhood other ways to handle frustration can be learned, but anger is often a healthy reaction throughout life.) Interestingly, early aggression among toddlers also is related directly to intentionality. It is object-centered, most commonly being physical assertiveness to obtain or retain an object, that is, to carry out an intent.[2] Aggression, too, emerges naturally. Its appearance is not unhealthy, though the child must be helped to handle such feelings in different ways.

When late in the first year the infant can carry out an intention and also be aware of (remember) a prohibition, one sees the sheepish facial expression and behavior I have termed *naughtiness.* I think this occurs only when a prohibition has been violated with a clear sense of intent. Much later, in the third or fourth years according to psychoanalytic theory, such a feeling is elaborated into guilt, the infant's clear feeling that he or she has done wrong, violated some standard. Joy, anger, aggression, and ultimately guilt all are related closely to the unfolding of intentionality.

Object Permanence and Memory

Object permanence is of vital importance in development. When the infant knows objects and persons exist even when not in view or physically present, intentionality can be extended dramatically.

---

[2]Dr. Wanda Bronson, Dept. of Personal Communication, University of California.

It can act with respect to objects with the anticipation of producing them, an important aspect of the developing future sense. And the desire to retrieve previously abandoned objects helps to expand the infant's memory capacity. To have *object permanence,* the infant must have some representation of the object in its mind.

Fear

The development of internal representation and the sense of permanence is related clearly to fear. For there to be a violation of expectation and therefore fear (or glee), there must be an expectation. One theory of stranger fear, for example, is that the infant looks to the stranger, expecting (wanting) to see a familiar face, but is unable to match the stranger's face with the internal representation of known faces. Especially when this occurs in an unfamiliar setting or in the absence of the caregiver, fear is likely during the second half-year of life. It is not so likely in the home or other secure context.

Another way of looking at fear is as a *categorical judgment.* Rather than a response to the unknown (which Gordon Bronson calls "wariness"), fear is a negative reaction to a class of events: "This is one of those and I don't like it." Such categorical reactions, of course, require categories, which depend on internal representation or memory. It is understandable that fear appears in the second half-year of life and expands into the toddler period as the capacity to form categories expands.

Anger

Object permanence and internal representation also relate to anger in that the infant will still desire an object that has become inaccessible, lost, or is not in its expected place. (Object permanence, persistence, and intentionality all are tied together.) Similarly, separation protest is accelerated, because out of sight does not mean out of mind.

Object (person) permanence is linked closely to attachment, also, which is the cornerstone of love (discussed below).

Imitation

You learned earlier that the development of imitation follows a series of stages as does object permanence, intentionality, and the ability to coordinate schemes. From behaviors perpetuated by general excitement to behaviors repeated following your repetition, the infant progresses in the second half-year of life to being able to imitate virtually any action, even though not witnessed before and even hours or days after he saw you do it (Figure 8-2).

Increasingly, imitative skill plays a role in the expression of emotions. Toddlers see and model your ways of expressing feelings. Even young infants sense your fearful and angry reactions, and they cry when other infants cry. Toddlers pick up your fears and learn to express anger and joy the way you do.

Differentiation of Persons and the Self

Development is an integrated process. Differentiation of persons and of the self draws on every aspect of development we have discussed. For example, the emergence of mother as a person, and ultimately the self as well, derives from the history of coordinated impressions of the mother over the first half-year of life and beyond. Acting on objects and persons, carrying through intentions with respect to them, is the foundation of the baby's sense of effectance and therefore of itself. You are what you do. You exist as a conscious being because you desire, and seek, and will. Object permanence and person permanence, of course, are tied closely to the sense that other persons exist separately from you. They come and go partly independent of your wishes.

Figure 8-2. By the end of the first year the baby can imitate things it saw you do sometime earlier; here, pat-a-cake. (Photo: P. LaSota.)

Differentiation of persons and the self begins with the original differentiation between the self and the surroundings (the "me" and the "out there"), which occurs in the first three months of life. The infant learns that some of his sensations originate outside of his body. Persons take on special salience and receive early smiles of recognition. They are part of the familiar in the "out there." Soon the infant is smiling differentially, that is, more to the caregiver than to unfamiliar persons. Differential experience produces differential responsiveness. Usually around the middle of the first year the infant stops smiling at strangers altogether when they are close at hand. This sug-

132

gests a rather advanced distinction. At about the same time the sense of the caregiver as a person is emerging, as a single source of the collection of impressions and experiences that emanate from him or her, as a complex entity that can come and go but continues to exist even when not present. Actual fear of strangers probably reflects a further differentiation of persons.

Throughout we have implied that the sense of self in part follows from "knowing" the other person as a person. Mother as she who touches me, bathes me, feeds me, and so on leads to I am he who is touched, bathed, and fed. Knowing and relating to people is important in defining the self, in infancy and throughout life.

As was the case with awareness of persons, we find evidence in the second half-year for the beginning awareness of the self. Early, for example at about seven months, the infant may peak in his delight in his mirror image. This is also a time when all parts of the body are being explored. Following this phase, sober and then shy or coy reactions to the mirror image appear. It is as though the infant is wondering, "Who is that? Is that me?" Other evidence suggests that true self-recognition occurs in the second year (Chapter 9).

The differentiation of persons and the self is central in the unfolding and/or expression of all the emotions. You know how such differentiation is involved in stranger fear. Likewise, according to our interpersonal definition, anger springs from the knowledge that the other *person* can interfere with *your* intent. The infant must have some sense of the other person as an entity, separate from him- or herself, to experience anger. At the same time, experiencing *you* as the source of the frustration, as not doing what *he* or *she* wants, helps the

Anger

infant to conceive of you as a separate, conscious being, just as does its seeing you as a means for achieving a goal. Cognitive development contributes to the evolution of emotion, and emotion contributes to cognitive development.

You also may recall from our discussion of laughter that in the second half-year laughter takes a clearly social turn. Games and incongruities involving the caregiver come to the fore. Games

Laughter involving transformations of the caregiver (cloth in mouth, mask, peekaboo, hiding) are especially funny. These all rest on some knowledge of the caregiver as a person. Laughter, of course, is very much a social behavior. It occurs primarily with others present, it is contagious, and it *communicates* well-being. The distinctive facial expressions associated with each emotion make clear that all emotions have a social–communicative component. Differentiation of the self and persons is also crucial in the development of the more advanced emotions such as shame, guilt, love, and empathy. These are discussed in Chapter 9.

Attachment

Attachment is related closely to the differentiation of persons. In fact, attachment refers specifically to selecting out a figure or figures and exhibiting patterns of behavior differentially with respect to her, him, or them. The infant will cling to the mother (or father) when distressed, keep check on her whereabouts, go to her when frightened, and use her as a secure base from which to explore. This selectivity implies the caregiver is distinguished from other people and has special significance. This specific affective tie is clear in the warm, **134** greeting behaviors, the expression of positive affect,

and the sharing of play between infant and caregiver (Figure 8-3). Such behaviors also indicate the
infant's attachment to the father and to siblings as
well, even though the attachment to the mother
may be primary.

Not surprisingly, research has shown that
solid attachments typically are not apparent until
the second half-year of life, when the infant differentiates persons to a considerable degree and
has a dawning sense of the self. In one sense your
infant "knows" you even during the newborn
period. It becomes used to your patterns of behaving, your voice and smell, and so on. Research
has shown that even during this early period infants
react to substitute caregivers and seem to "recognize" the regular care of mother. Louis Sander
has described this type of knowing in comparison
to the knowing we would speak of during the
second half-year: "It is to be noted that the hypothe-
sized recognitory processes are not conceptualized
in terms of the psychological recognition of the
mother. Rather it is considered to be a biological
recognition process, which serves as the *anlage*
for the later development of person recognition"
(presentation at the Society for Research in Child
Development).

One may think of the first six months as the
period in which the foundations for the attachment
relationship are being established. Through interaction, the prerequisite experience for person permanence is being acquired, and the caregiver is
becoming familiar to the infant. At the same time
the caregiver is learning the infant's signal system
and preferences and is learning to tune to the
infant. This learning by both infant and caregiver
is vital for the formation of attachment. Still,
loss of the caregiver in the first half-year is *rela-*

Figure 8-3. This infant's exuberant greeting of her arriving father not only expresses the attachment bond, it reveals important mental development. The caregiver is immediately recognized and assimilated to a positively-toned scheme. The baby is happy to see him. (Photo: P. LaSota.)

tively nondisruptive (though loss and even prolonged separations always may be serious). If there is another available attachment figure, the infant will form an attachment. If this person is available for the kind of learning just described, the attachment relationship can be a good one.

Following the formation of attachment in the second half-year of life, disruption of the relationship has serious negative consequences. When separations are brief there may be the familiar protest or sometimes what might better be called **Anxiety** *anxiety*. The attachment figure is an important source of familiarity and security, and separation from her or him is threatening. In fact, many theorists consider separation to be the *prototype* of anxiety, the basic core of all later experiences of anxiety. With development the fear of literal separation can evolve to fear of disapproval or loss of love and even self-disapproval and loss of the self (*existential anxiety*). The security of the early attachment relationship may in a very basic way influence the tendency to be a basically anxious person or to face experience with a tolerable degree of anxiety. If the infant is constantly uncertain about the availability (physical or psychological) of the attachment figure, it later may be uncertain about the availability of its own resources. (More is said about this in the next two chapters.)

More prolonged separations (for example, hospitalization of the mother) will produce a more extreme reaction that may be divided into the three stages of protest, despair, and detachment. Following a period of great distress, the infant appears to be both distressed and apathetic. Finally, it no longer seems to care and becomes somewhat more responsive to others. That this detachment is still part of the separation reaction, and not early recovery, is indicated by the infant's behavior if reunited with the mother at this point. It selectively ignores or actively avoids her. It behaves as though it did not know her, though less significant individuals are recognized. In time, the infant traces the path back through these steps. It becomes actively, directly angry, protests a great deal, and is very demanding of comforting. Ultimately, the harmonious, preseparation relationship again may be established. These sequences of behavior indicate the strength of the affective bond between the attached infant and its caregiver and the great complexity of infant emotional behavior.

Detachment

Finally, actual loss of the attachment figure, which would be experienced by the infant even in a very prolonged separation, produces the reaction of grief. Only with the formation of attachment can there be grief. Certainly, even in the first half-year, permanent separation from the caregiver can lead to a negative reaction. An important part of the infant's routine and continuity has been upset. But only when there is the *experience of*

Grief

loss can there be grief. To experience loss the infant must have in some sense become tied together with the caregiver. The infant has in a sense lost a part of the self.

It is interesting that differentiation of persons is required for attachment to occur and for these important separation reactions to develop. The infant must have some sense of the caregiver as a separate, specific person, as well as some sense of the self. It is also true, of course, that the attachment relationship promotes the processes of differentiation of persons and definition of the self and that attachment formation and differentiation go forward together. Some even have suggested that the experiences of separation anxiety (in moderate amounts) are crucial for the birth of the self, that they lead to an awareness of separateness.[3] It is not so much differentiation, *then* attachment, as differentiation *and* attachment. More is said about this in the next two chapters.

Love

This joining together of infant and caregiver not only makes possible loss and grief; it is the very cornerstone of love. Professor Harlow was not being facetious when he titled his article about the attachment of infant monkeys to their cloth substitute mother "The Nature of Love." His studies revealed the superordinate importance of physical closeness and contact (the merging of the infant monkey with the "mother" figure) over simply being fed. The attraction of these monkeys to their mother substitute, of course, was not love; nor is the attachment of the infant to its caregiver. Love is more than a sense of security or a trust in having one's needs met. Love involves mutual

[3]Brody and Axelrod, 1970.

empathy. It involves giving and caring for and about the other. Infants in the first year of life are capable of neither empathy nor love. But the capacity to tie the self to another, to develop a sense of trust of the other, and even vulnerability concerning separation are foundations of later love relationships. Erik Erikson has written of how the sense of trust lays the groundwork for the sense of trustworthiness. Similarly, the sense of being loved and lovable is the foundation for the ability to love.

Summary

As you have seen, all of the critical themes of development have a turning point in the second half-year of life. At the same time, there is a dramatic differentiation of the emotions from general distress and early pleasure to unhappiness, fear, anger, grief, and the varieties of joy. There are beginning differentiations of persons and the self, and the attachment bond is formed. Developmentally advanced emotions—shame and guilt, empathy and love—will appear later, but they clearly have their origins in this period as well (Chapter 9). This is not to say that the second half-year of life is more important than the first half-year. Within a developmental point of view, such a statement is absurd. There is a critical reorganization and rapid unfolding in the second half-year, but the shadows of these developmental themes are seen even in the newborn period. And the roots are laid out in the first half-year, at which time there is the basic differentiation of the self from the surroundings, paving the way for all further development.

Sources

AINSWORTH, M. The development of infant–mother attachment. In B. Caldwell & H. Ricciuti (Eds.), *Review of child development research. Vol. 3.* Chicago: University of Chicago Press, 1974.

BRODY, S., & AXELROD, S. *Anxiety and ego formation in infancy.* New York: International Universities Press, 1970.

BRONSON, G., & PANKEY, W. On the distinction between wariness and fear. *Child Development,* in press.

BÜHLER, C., *The first year of life.* New York: The John Day Co., 1930.

HARLOW, H., & ZIMMERMANN, R. Affectional responses in the infant monkey. *Science,* 1959, *130,* 421–32.

SANDER, L. Issues in early mother–child interaction. *Journal of the American Academy of Child Psychiatry,* 1962, *1,* 141–66.

SROUFE, L. A. The ontogenesis of the emotions. In J. Osofsky (Ed.), *Handbook of infant development.* New York: John Wiley and Sons, Inc., in press.

SROUFE, L. A., & MITCHELL, P. Emotional development. In J. Osofsky (Ed.), *Handbook of infant development.* New York: John Wiley and Sons, Inc., in press.

SROUFE, L. A., & WUNSCH, J. P. The development of laughter in the first year of life. *Child Development,* 1972, *43,* 1326–44.

9

The Emergence of the Autonomous Self

The child is developing in several areas at the same time. He learns to walk, to climb, and later to run. Simultaneously, he is developing increased manual dexterity. In the intellectual area, he begins to manipulate action symbols and, later, internalized images. Language skills burst forth. . . . All of these increases in competence combine . . . to produce . . . an overemphasis on his new independence. This is characterized by overdoing newly-discovered skills; by refusing to comply with parental demands and by insisting on doing things "by myself"; and by insisting on having things his own way. . . .

As the child pushes his independence to its limits, he is forced to rely on those techniques within his capabilities. Since parents frustrate his wishes by saying "no" to him, and since [the toddler's] thought rests largely on the imitation of gestures, it is only natural that he turn their "no's" against them. This is part of the negativistic behavior that is so typical of the period from one and a half to three or three and a half.

BREGER, *From Instinct to Identity*

By the second quarter of the first year, the infant experiences the first genuine emotions—the pleasure smile of recognition, distress in the face of the   141 unfamiliar (wariness), and rage or disappointment when a specific action or interaction is stopped. These are true emotions, because they represent *a connection between the infant and its world.* The reaction is in response to a *particular* event and depends in large part on psychological processes within the infant. The dangling clown, for example, produces smiling after several presentations. If a novel object is substituted, smiling is postponed or stopped, had it begun already. The infant smiles because of effortful recognition of *this* object, not because of the stimulation by any object placed in front of it.

It is in this sense that we can say there is a dawning of awareness in the third month; that is, there is a basic distinction between the "in-here" and the "out-there." And it is because the reaction reflects a relation between the subject and the event that we can infer the emotion of pleasure. A baby seeing the clown for the first time probably will not smile. Emotional reactions always imply a connection between the child and the event, the involvement of psychological rather than merely physiological processes. The presence of such emotional reactions by the third month is what led René Spitz to refer to this period as the "birth of the Ego." They represent the first step toward the development of the self.

But it is not until about the beginning of the fourth quarter of the first year that the infant is an *emotional being.* By this time the infant may experience threat *in advance* of noxious stimulation (fear). It may be angry when an obstacle blocks an *intended* act. And it laughs even *before* mother's return in peekaboo. In a new way the meaning of the event for the infant determines the affect. Awareness has become anticipation.

The baby can expect to get the ball from under the chair (though it never has reached there before), and it can be surprised or even angry at the result.

The ten-month-old is also an emotional being, because its schemes or memories are affectively colored. This is why upon a parent's arrival home from work one sees the bouncing, smiling, squealing greeting (Figure 8-3). The baby does not need to figure out who this is and decide how it feels about seeing her or him. Rather, the attachment figure immediately is linked (assimilated) to a special, positively toned scheme. *The baby is happy to see you.* Similarly, seeing a person in a white coat following a trip to the doctor for shots can produce an immediate fear reaction. Again, the ten-month-old does not need to ponderously evaluate this event. It does not like it.

There is another important way in which we can say that the infant is an emotional being by the fourth quarter. There is a new level of awareness, an awareness of the affect itself. By this time the infant's own affective reactions influence its further behavior. Rather than terminating an interaction with the environment, affect now forecasts behavior. The infant laughs as it begins stuffing the cloth in your mouth, and its angry or fearful expression tells you it is going to flail at the obstacle or avoid the threat. Moreover, previous affective reactions become part of its continuing appraisal of situations. If it was distressed by your brief separation, it is now more sensitive to your movements, even though it seems contented in your presence.

As you no doubt expect, important developments continue to occur rapidly in the second year of life. By early in the second year the infant is capable of *moods* (elation, sadness, petulance), **143** and its *prevailing affective state* provides a context for its behavior. Sometimes this will delight you, and sometimes it will be unbelievably trying. At this point in development the infant has the capacity to be joyous on merely entering a new play arena or going "outside." It also has the capacity to be cranky, despite your talent for distraction; but as is discussed in Chapter 10, early in the second year the negative periods are typically brief.

The further development of memory and beginning language help to provide a basis for greatly expanded coping skills in the second year. By this period you will see your baby holding back and even fighting back tears and being much more fluid in its emotional reactions; for example, it can stop crying to take in more information. It can better tolerate separations and ultimately can make use of your verbal reassurances to deal with feelings aroused by brief separations. It has increasingly varied means to express feelings and to reestablish contact with you. Over the course of the second year, less *physical* contact will be required for comforting. Verbal, affective, and interactive sharing typically begin substituting for physical contact.

There are also important advances in the formation (differentiation) of the self during the second year. The infant is aware not only of the "out-there" and of its own feelings, it also becomes aware of the self as experiencing and the self as actor. Spitz speaks of the beginning formation of the Ego or self at three months, Brody and Axelrod later in the first year with the onset of separation anxiety. Clearly, one can speak of the emergence of the self or the person at many points in development. And the most appropriate view, in my opinion, is to think of the self as emerg*ing,* rather than emerg*ent,* a process that continues throughout the life span. Still, if one wishes to pick one age at which the self has emerged, the most persuasive case can be made for the second year. It is during this time that there is evidence for self-recognition, self-assertion ("I do it"), and feelings about the self.

Some Major Developments of the Second Year

Perhaps the major general developments of the second year are in the areas of representation and language, self–other differentiation, and mobility. Symbolic labels and beginning language, of course, are great aids for the developing memory. During this year your baby will be able to find objects on request and will be able to retrieve an object when it is needed in current play; for example, it can go and get its toy horse when playing with the barn. It can carry out an action it saw someone else do some time before. And it can recall how it solved a problem previously.

This is also the year in which it becomes quite competent at getting wherever it wants to get. Its motor skills now will include walking and moving furniture to assist its climbing activities, and this motoric skill combines with and contributes to an "experimental" attitude. Your baby will be exploring everything, investigating everything, and *into everything.* This is an incredibly active year.

The motor and representational skills and the active venturing forth into the world converge to promote the discovery of the self. The child becomes the central permanent object—the principal constancy amidst the changing experience. You are what you do. In the second year the infant does a

145

great deal and does it on its own. Its operating in separation from the caregiver inevitably leads it to a recognition of *its* actions and to an awareness of itself as separate.

There is evidence for this, and some of it will be quite clear to you. This is the age at which willfulness and self-assertion become apparent. "No" will be an early word, and it will appear even earlier as a gesture. As soon as phrases are established, "I do it" and "do it myself" will appear; and even before that your infant will let you know in very clear ways when it does not want your interference. It also is letting you know that it is becoming a toddler (Figure 9-1).

Usually by fifteen to eighteen months, infants also provide clear evidence of self-recognition. By the end of the first year they looked coyly into a mirror. In the middle of the second year when you

Figure 9-1. "Do it myself." (Photo: G. Sroufe.)

unobtrusively smear rouge onto their nose, then show them the mirror, they immediately will reach their hand to their nose.[1] They know the smudge is on *them,* not the "baby in the mirror." Shortly after this time, of course, some will name themselves when looking in the mirror.

Emotions of the Toddler Period

The emergence of the autonomous self has clear implications for the development of emotions (see Table 9-1). At the same time, the very appearance of certain emotions gives testimony to the further differentiation of the self in the second year. Shame, affection, and defiance all reflect a considerable degree of differentiation of the infant from its caregivers; that is, they indicate that the infant is becoming a unique being, separate from you. Earlier the infant may be angry at you, as it is at any obstacle. But in the second year it may be angry for something you no longer are doing, and it may defiantly pit its wishes against yours. At times your very request is sufficient to produce such negativism. The child also may tantrum with a persistence and intensity that is something to behold. This is what is meant by the "terrible two's."

Defiance

From Affection to Love

While the attachment relationship is formed in the first year, we were interested in our research to note that spontaneous love pats and other signs of affection do not become common until the second year. This makes sense. As the infant

Affection

[1]Observation by Dr. Amsterdam and by Drs. Lewis and Brooks.

recognizes the personness of the attachment figure and is aware of its connection to that person, it can have the positive feelings we call affection (Figure 9-2). It also can experience positive valuations of the self, especially when praised; that is, the baby can be pleased with itself.

Love
Pride

Considerably later, love and pride will evolve from the affection and positive self-evaluation of this period. Both love and pride involve a further differentiation of the self. Pride, for example, involves a sense of responsibility for one's acts, the achievement of standards that the child has adopted. This is beyond the capacity of the toddler.

An idea that interests me very much is that intimacy or love involves the fusion of *separate* persons. The more complete the differentiation (independence) of the persons, the more complete can be the fusion; and the more complete the differentiation and fusion, the deeper is the love. Thus, at each stage of life there is more individuation (establishing the self as a separate person) and more capacity for joining with another. For example, only at about age four, when a rather complete separating (individuating) from the caregivers is a major developmental task, does identification emerge. The child goes beyond simple imitation of behaviors and strives *to be like* the parent. In a sense, the child incorporates the parent into the self, or as I prefer to think of it, joins with the parent in a more complete way. This may be the first age at which the child loves. And, according to Erikson, only after adolescence, when a rather complete sense of self-identity is achieved (i.e., knowing the self as a separate entity), is true intimacy possible. Intimacy with another will, of course, further elaborates the sense of identity. The capability for love, the most complex and advanced emotion, continues to develop at every stage of life; but it has its roots in infancy and childhood.

Figure 9-2. By the beginning of the second year, the infant shows and shares things it sees or finds with the caregiver. Such sharing is the beginning of an affectionate relationship on the part of the infant. (Photo: R. Cooper.)

From Shame to Guilt

In Erik Erikson's writing, shame refers to the feeling of the self being exposed, seen—the dirty self. Not *what you did* but *you* are bad. It is the opposite of the positive self-evaluation. As such, shame is only possible with the emergence of the autonomous self, and it may be the most clear indication that the child has self-awareness, self-consciousness. Shame is not one of my favorite emotions, and I think pervasive feelings of shame are the basis for much psychological disturbance. All children will experience shame, however, and it emerges according to developmental laws as do all the other affects. Since the child is most susceptible to shame when the self is newly formed, this is a time of vulnerability. Fortunately, a baby you have enjoyed

Shame

will have learned to enjoy and like himself or
herself. And a baby you enjoy, *you* are not likely
to shame; so experiences of shame will be infrequent and short-lived.

As love and pride required a rather complete
differentiation of the self, so too does guilt require
further self-differentiation to evolve from shame
during the preschool years. Guilt like pride involves
a sense of responsibility for one's acts. It reflects a
violation of the child's standards, a violation of the
internalized parental prohibitions. Whereas shame
Guilt is the sense of being exposed (caught), guilt is the
anticipation of punishment or more—the belief
that one should be punished. Not being seen but
the very act itself is sufficient to produce the
negative feeling, because the loss of approval now
resides in the self. Guilt is also a product of identification, and it is related to fear, anger, shame,
and self-love in a complex way.

From Imitation to Empathy

Part of the self–other differentiation is role-taking.
Role-taking means understanding—first, that the
other person has a perspective, has an experience,
and second, some idea of what that perception or
experience would be in a particular situation. Role-
Empathy taking has its roots in imitation. As the infant
imitates the actions and later the affective expressions of others, it begins to learn that others see
and feel and behave in ways like it does. Role-
taking is, of course, also dependent upon the
sense of separateness from the other. It both depends upon and contributes to such an under-
150 standing.

Role-taking along with well-developed intentionality produces the very beginnings of empathy in the second year. Work by Wanda Bronson has shown that when toddlers see another child striving for a goal, perhaps trying to reach an object, they sometimes will help them achieve the goal (push the object toward them). In the second year, it is not likely that this is true empathy. The child of eighteen months probably cannot truly get inside another's skin. But it does see what the other child is *intending* with enough clarity that it seeks closure on the same act. This is certainly the beginnings of empathetic understanding. By age two the child may turn its doll toward the page when showing it pictures in a book.

Emotions and the Differentiation of the Self

It is important to repeat here a basic idea within developmental psychology: development is an integrative process. It is certainly true that differentiation of the self has consequences for the unfolding of the emotions, and so does identification with the caregivers. It is also true, however, that affective experience contributes to these aspects of cognitive and social development. *Feelings* of shame and pride promote self-awareness. In many ways such feelings *are* self-awareness. Similarly, feelings of affection, closeness, and love, and even feelings of separateness and defiance promote the process of identification. Your infant and you are tied together by the feelings you have toward each other and share with each other.

Summary: Age of Onset
of the Basic Emotions

There is actually very little reliable information on the emergence of the various emotions, especially anger and the developmentally advanced emotions, but Table 9-1 represents a reasonable working scheme at present. Ages given are, of course, only tentative and approximate.

In this scheme the emotions are grouped into three unfolding systems, pleasure–joy, wariness–fear, and rage–anger. For example, in the wariness–fear system, distress due to being startled or to pain is transformed to distress due to "obligatory attention," crying that occurs in the early weeks when the infant is frozen in contact with some stimulation. (Stoppage of behavior apparently leads to a build-up in arousal and then distress.) Later this evolves to *wariness* ("fear" of the unfamiliar) when the behavioral arrest is due to the *specific content* of the event—the mixture of familiar and unfamiliar elements. This is genuine emotion. Wariness evolves to fear proper, where the event has a negative *meaning* for the infant, and later to shame and guilt. Guilt also is related to anger that evolves from rage. Affection, love, and pride are tied to the pleasure–joy system (see Table 9-1).

You may notice some very interesting parallels among the three systems. The first true emotions within each system (pleasure, wariness, and rage due to disappointment of terminating a specific action) all are seen to emerge at about the same time, three to four months, when the reaction is the result of a specific event. Likewise, joy, fear, and anger are seen to emerge in the third quarter, when the *meaning* of the event becomes central. Elation, anxiety, and angry mood emerge by the end of the first year. Later, shame, affection, and defiance emerge at the same time, as do pride, love, and guilt. The accuracy of this scheme is yet to be fully confirmed. Still, you may find it a useful guide in observing your child's development.

Table 9-1:   The Ontogenesis of Some Basic Human Emotions

Month	Pleasure–Joy	Wariness–Fear	Rage–Anger
0	endogenous smile	startle/pain	distress due to:
			covering the face, physical restraint,
1	turning toward	obligatory attention	extreme discomfort
2			rage
3	pleasure		(disappointment)
4	delight	wariness	
5	active laughter		
6			
7	joy		anger
8			
9		fear (stranger aversion)	
10			
11			
12	elation	anxiety immediate fear	angry mood, petulance
18	positive valuation of self affection	shame	defiance
24			intentional hurting
36	pride, love		guilt

Sources

BREGER, L. *From instinct to identity: The development of personality.* Englewood Cliffs, N.J.: Prentice-Hall, Inc., 1974.

BRODY, S., & AXELROD, S. *Anxiety and ego formation in infancy.* New York: International Universities Press, 1970.

153

BRONSON, W. Mother–toddler interaction: A perspective on studying the development of competence. *Merrill–Palmer Quarterly*, 1974, *20*, 275–300.

EMDE, R., GAENSBAUER, T., & HARMON, R. Emotional expression in infancy: A biobehavioral study. *Psychological Issues Monograph Series*, 1976.

ERIKSON, E. *Childhood and society*. New York: Norton & Co., 1950.

LEWIS, M., & BROOKS, J. Self-knowledge and emotional development. In M. Lewis and L. Rosenblum (Eds.), *The origins of behavior: Affect development*. New York: Plenum Press, in press.

MAHLER, M. *The psychological birth of the infant*. New York: Basic Books, 1975.

SPITZ, R., EMDE, R., & METCALF, L. Further prototypes of ego formation. *Psychoanalytic Study of the Child*, 1970, *25*, 417–44.

SROUFE, L. A. The ontogenesis of the emotions. In J. Osofsky (Ed.), *Handbook of infant development*. New York: John Wiley and Sons, Inc., in press.

SROUFE, L. A., & MITCHELL, P. Emotional development. In J. Osofsky (Ed.), *Handbook of infant development*. New York: John Wiley and Sons, Inc., in press.

10

The Roots of Personality

The loving mother teaches her child to walk alone. She is far enough from him so that she cannot actually support him, but she holds out her arms to him. She imitates his movements, and if he totters, she swiftly bends as if to seize him, so that the child might believe that he is not walking alone. . . . And yet, she does more. Her face beckons like a reward, an encouragement. Thus, the child walks alone with his eyes fixed on his mother's face, not on the difficulties in his way. He supports himself by the arms that do not hold him and constantly strives towards the refuge in his mother's embrace, little suspecting that in the very same moment that he is emphasizing his need of her, he is proving that he can do without her, because he is walking alone.

Soren Kierkegaard*

Your baby's psychological growth can be described in yet another way, in terms of periods (stages) of social–emotional development. These periods, in addition to revealing the nature of the developmental process, reflect the central tasks or issues

*From *Purity of heart is to will one thing* (p. 85). Trans. Douglas V. Steere. Copyright 1938, 1948 by Harper and Row, Publishers, Inc. Reprinted by permission of the publisher.

facing infant and caregiver. Such developmental issues provide an important context for viewing the caregiver–infant relationship and the beginning formation of personality. It is my belief that by the preschool years your child is in many ways the person he or she is going to be. There is much you can do to promote healthy development during these critical early years.

To me it makes sense to look at social and emotional development as passing through a series of phases. These developmental periods do not have the status of formal stages; that is, it is not established that this is a necessary sequence for all babies. Still, it seems possible and useful to summarize development across spans of time longer than weeks or months and to divide the periods in terms of developmental accomplishments or tasks or issues. Such a summary captures the swelling and receding nature of emotional development. It seems to be the case that the periods of expansiveness inevitably lead the infant to new challenges or crises. When these are to some extent resolved, new periods of expansiveness follow in the continuing wake of development. Such periods of development are tied closely to the separation-individuation process, the child's becoming a person separate from its caregivers.

The Course of Affective Development

In Table 10-1 are listed a tentative series of steps in the course of affective (emotional) development. For comparative purposes I also have included the social development sequence proposed by Louis Sander and Piaget's stages of cognitive development. These three schemes prove to be coordinated remarkably, given that they were developed largely independent of one another and from examining different aspects of behavior. As you read this chapter you may wish to consult this table occasionally and to compare it with Table 9-1.

During the initial period of life (the "absolute stimulus barrier") the infant is relatively invulnerable to external stimulation. By contrast, in the second period (a "turning toward," roughly one to three months) it shows a greatly increased interest in and receptivity to stimulation. It is awake and alert more and has a greatly increased capacity for sustained attention. The infant is relatively vulnerable during this phase, since its capacities for tension regulation are limited. It does develop the ability to coordinate attention, motor activity, and positive affect (smiling and cooing) so that tension can be regulated through positive discharge. By two months it stills and looks, then kicks and waves its arms with smiling, then attends again. It also has its caregivers to protect it from overstimulation. Sander points to a vital initial function of the caregivers, helping the infant with early physiological regulation. You can do this by establishing smooth and harmonious routines.

The reliable social smile ushers in the "period of positive affect" (three to six months). During this period there is awareness, and there are motor expectations and attempts to repeat actions. There can be disappointment, failures of assimilation, and frustration. Therefore, in addition to pleasure, there can be negative emotions such as rage and wariness. But the predominant tone of this period typically will be positive. Your baby will be delightful to you and to others. The baby will be able to exercise many general schemes (for example, reaching) without disruption and to its great satisfaction. Its smiles and generally greater responsivity will draw you closer, and its positive responses to your initiatives will be very gratifying. Now the infant has the capacity to actively avoid noxious stimulation so that it is less often distressed and, probably based on maturation, infantile fussiness (so-called colic) disappears. "The infant smiles and coos at its own feet, at its toy giraffe and especially at its caregivers. For the first time it *laughs* in response to vigorous stimulation. . . . With sparkling eyes, caregiver and infant set out upon the task of establishing reciprocal exchanges."[1] This is the period in which the playful interactions described in Chapter 6 become crucial. Your infant is receptive to such exchanges, and they promote further cognitive, affective, and social growth. Here are the roots of reciprocity, the beginning sense of give and take between infant and caregiver.

Many observers again agree in describing the next period as a time of *active* engagement and mastery. With budding intentionality the baby produces consequences in its environment and actively explores the person of its caregivers. I call it the "period of active participation" (six to nine months). The social explosion of this age surpasses even that of the preceding period. This is the age when laughter to social games becomes prominent. Such laughter signifies the greater participation of the infant in its experience; it is no longer what you do to her or him but what the two of you do together that is so effective in producing laughter. At the same time, the baby much more commonly initiates the interaction. It now will vocalize, touch, cajole, or otherwise try to get a response from you, a sibling, or, quite strikingly, a visiting baby. "As there is increasing meaning in the infant's trans-

---

158 [1]Sroufe, L. A. The ontogenesis of emotion in infancy, in press.

able 10-1: Stages of Cognitive Development and Related Changes in the Affective and Social Domains

Cognitive Development: Piaget	Affective Development: Sroufe	Social Development: Sander
0-1 Use of Reflexes [A]nimal generalization/accom-odation of inborn behaviors.	*0-1 Absolute Stimulus Barrier* *built-in protection	*0-3 Initial Regulation* *sleeping, feeding, quieting, arousal *beginning preferential responsiveness to caregiver
[1]-4 Primary Circular Reaction [fi]rst acquired adaptations (centered on body) [an]ticipation based on visual cues [be]ginning coordination of schemes	*1-3 Turning Toward* *orientation to external world *relative vulnerability to stimulation *exogenous (social) smile	
[4]-8 Secondary Circular Reaction [be]havior directed toward external world (sensorimotor "classes" and cognition) [be]ginning goal orientation (procedures for making interesting sights last, deferred circular reactions)	*3-6 Positive Affect* *content-mediated affect (pleasurable assimilation, failure to assimilate, disappointment, frustration) *pleasure as an excitatory process (laughter, social responsivity) *active stimulus barrier (investment and divestment of affect)	*4-6 Reciprocal Exchange* *mother and child coordinate feeding, caretaking activities *affective, vocal, and motor play
	7-9 Active Participation *joy at being a cause (mastery, initiation of social games) *failure of intended acts (experience of interruption) *differentiation of emotional reactions (initial hesitancy, positive and negative social responses, and categories)	*7-9 Initiative* *early directed activity (infant initiates social exchange, preferred activities) *experience of success or interference in achieving goals
[8]-12 Coordination of Secondary Schemes & Application to New Situations [o]bjectification of the world (interest in object qualities & relations, search for hidden objects) [tr]ue intentionality (means-ends differentiation, tool-using) [i]mitation of novel responses [be]ginning appreciation of causal relations (others seen as agents, anticipation of consequences)	*9-12 Attachment* *affectively toned schemes (specific affective bond, categorical reactions) *integration and coordination of emotional reactions (context-mediated responses, including evaluation and beginning coping functions)	*10-13 Focalization* *mother's availability and responsivity tested (demands focused on mother) *exploration from secure base *reciprocity dependent on contextual information
[1]2-18 Tertiary Circular Reaction [p]ursuit of novelty (active experimentation to provoke new effects) [tr]ial-and-error problem solving (invention of new means) [p]hysical causality spatialized & detached from child's actions	*12-18 Practicing* *caregiver the secure base for exploration *elation in mastery *affect as part of context (moods, stored or delayed feelings) *control of emotional expression	*14-20 Self-Assertion* *broadened initiative *success and gratification achieved apart from mother
[1]8-24 Invention of New Means Through Mental Combination [s]ymbolic representation (language, deferred imitation, symbolic play) [p]roblem solving without overt action (novel combinations of schemes)	*18-36 Emergence of Self-Concept* *sense of self as actor (active coping, positive self-evaluation, shame) *sense of separateness (affection, ambivalence, conflict of wills, defiance)	

actions with the surround, emotional reactions become more differentiated in this phase, with an initial hesitancy in the face of novel objects and sober faces for strangers. Joy, fear and anger are its products."[2]

During the "period of attachment" (Period 5), an exclusive preoccupation with the caregiver may develop, along with an intensification of negative reactions to strangers and a temporarily subdued affective tone. It is not at all that the baby becomes generally negative. This is when the vigorous and delightful positive greeting responses typically emerge, and there is still a great deal of smiling and laughter in social games, with the infant being very active in these (e.g., stuffing the cloth back in your mouth). Rather than being generally negative, the infant's emotions have become highly differentiated. The infant may be delightful when interacting with you, but for a time it also may cry whenever you leave the room and may show distress when strangers attempt to pick it up, especially when you are not present. This is simply part of the attachment process with some infants. They know *you* now and want to be with you, especially when distressed, ill, or upset. Other babies are generally receptive of strangers, but they still will show a preference for you when they are distressed. Such preference for you does not mean you have spoiled your baby; it means you are a source of security for them. By the end of this period you will see moods, ambivalence, and gradations of feeling, and there will be rather clear communication of emotion.

The infant again is filled with enthusiasm and confidence in the "practicing period" (twelve to

[2]*Ibid.*

eighteen months). This is the age of *exploration* and *experimentation.* The infant is into everything as it actively masters the inanimate world. It uses you as a base for exploration, retreating when necessary. But in the absence of threat or distress, it is off into the wonderful world of toys and objects, manipulating them, taking them apart, and combining them. As when your baby grinned on pushing itself to its hands and toes at seven or eight months, it is delighted and even cocky with the first steps

However, this sense of well-being and rather complete sense of confidence cannot endure un-now (Figure 10-1). It walks and later runs from you, laughing uproariously.

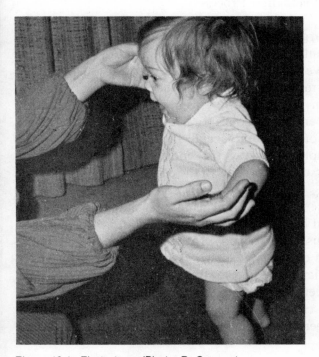

Figure 10-1. First steps. (Photo: R. Cooper.)

challenged. Moving out into the world inevitably and necessarily leads the infant to a sense of separateness from you. This is a temporary but necessary step in the "formation of the self-concept" (eighteen to twenty-four months). "To maintain the new-found sense of autonomy in the face of anxiety over separation and the increasing awareness of its limited power is the emotional task of the 2 year old, a task which is ultimately resolved with the development of 'play and fantasy' skills and later identification (period 8)."[3]

The Separation–Individuation Process

Margaret Mahler has proposed a series of developmental stages that are quite parallel to those we have been discussing. Her central theme is the formation of the self—the infant becoming an individual separate from the caregiver. Like my scheme, this conceptualization involves cognitive, emotional, and social factors, though here the emphasis is on the most fundamental social-personality process in the early years.

In agreement with Spitz and others, Mahler describes the infant as at first making no distinction between the external world and its own sensations. Its own body, the mother's body and voice, and everything else are part of the same, undifferentiated experience. Interestingly, when everything is centered in the "self," there is no self. While we can, of course, never know what the infant experiences, it does seem clear that its own internal

[3]*Ibid.*

sensations dominate in the early weeks and that it becomes more responsive to a particularized surrounding later.

It is interesting that the first step toward becoming an individual is becoming one with the caregiver(s). The infant makes the distinction between the in-here and the out-there, but it faces the out-there from within the security of what we call the attachment relationship. Mahler talks of this as the dual–unity (roughly three to ten months) to emphasize the way the infant and the caregiver are tied together completely. The infant does not know that the caregiver is not simply an extension of itself.

In the "practicing" phase (ten to eighteen months) the infant moves out from the caregiver and in so doing discovers its separateness and the caregiver's independence from it. Notice that as in the introductory quotation for this chapter, *the very security of the earlier closeness promotes the moving apart.*

Awareness of separateness inevitably leads the young toddler to a major conflict. The closeness of the dual–unity that it earlier experienced beckons. This is a great deal to leave behind. At the same time, it has a strong desire to maintain and assert its newfound autonomy. The attraction of the ever-expanding world is also powerful. The resolution of this conflict, and the name of this phase, is "rapprochement," a coming together of the infant and the caregiver in a new way. As discussed earlier, the separation–individuation process continues throughout the preschool period (and, of course, life), with a peak being reached by about age four, with identification. By this age, the child is no longer you; but you remain in a way within your child.

Your Relationship and the Crises of Early Development

This process view of the early development of the individual reveals a clear role for a good quality relationship between infant and caregivers. The security of the attachment promotes exploration and mastery of the object world. Since its energy is not tied up completely with you, it therefore is freed for other pursuits. The haven you provide when it is threatened, injured, or stressed also promotes exploration; and the sharing of its play with you is part of this mastery process. Its interests in objects and play does not completely cut it off from you but rather offers a new, more advanced way for being connected with you (Figure 10-2). The affective bond remains but at the same time is in a sense transferred to the object world. There is clearly an intrinsic interest in objects, but affective sharing with you enriches the quality of play (see again Figure 9-1).

The security of attachment influences the quality of exploration and play during the "practicing" phase. Similarly, there are at least two ways that the quality of this latter adaptation is important for the infant's handling of the rapprochement crisis. First, to the extent that exploration is interesting and gratifying and to the extent that mastery skills, confidence, and competence with objects are developed, the pull of the outer world will be strong. Development is its own impetus. The child will feel strong urges to go on developing new skills and encountering new experiences, and this will more than balance his wishes for the former type of closeness with his caregivers. At the same time, the caregiver's faithfulness in being available for comforting when the infant is

164

distressed and the caregiver's enjoyment of play and sharing experiences with the infant help it to know that contact will not be lost as it moves away. The bond is intact; it is merely transformed.

You probably cannot avoid the crisis of the second year, no matter how well you handle the early months. Chances are your infant will exhibit negativism, tantrums, and perhaps even periods of clingingness. This conflict is a normal part of development. However, as intense as the negativism may be at times, this period can be relatively brief and certainly noncatastrophic. Individual tantrums can be managed and the period can be weathered.[4] You have built the basis of confidence and trust in the first year. Because you have a history of reliability, your baby will more quickly accept the limits you now set on its uncontrolled behavior. At the same time, learning that you will be there to provide boundaries when it cannot control its own behavior will deepen its trust in you.

It is important that you not demand independence too early but that you accept the infant's moving out when it is time. Promoting precocious independence actually may lead to a poverty of exploration and play and may jeopardize the security of the attachment relationship. The secure attachment is the foundation for secure, independent functioning. Our research shows clearly that securely attached babies explore eagerly, develop adequate mastery skills, and approach problems with confidence in their second year. They are neither clingy nor *unduly* negativistic, and their negativism is balanced by an obvious ability to use the caregiver for support and assist-

---

[4] I recommend holding the child closely to you during a tantrum. That way you not only contain the tantrum, you also communicate your continued closeness.

Figure 10-2. The affective bond remains, but there is a new, more advanced way of being connected with you. (Photo: G. Sroufe)

ance. At the same time, you must not hold your baby back but rather must accept its increasing independence. You too must know that *you* are not losing your baby; you are helping your child unfold. Your relationship too is intact.

I do not wish to raise large worries in all this. First of all, your baby will help you with this a great deal. It is going to move out. And its increased interest in exploration and other autonomous activity will signal you clearly. Also, since you enjoyed your young infant, you will be very likely to enjoy your toddler as well. As a toddler it will be much more capable of sharing with you.

The father or second caregiver may have a special role in dealing with this crisis. Throughout this book the word *caregiver* has been used where you might have expected the word *mother*. This is because infants also may be securely attached to their fathers or to other adults sharing in their care (see Figure 8-3). There are many ways people can divide up the infant-rearing task. However, even in families where the mother has primary responsibility for the infant's care and is the primary attachment figure, the second caregiver can play a vital role. It is important that this second person

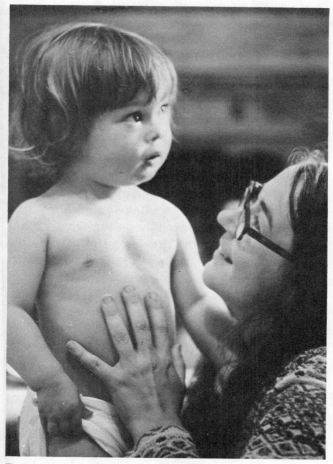

Figure 10-3. You are helping your child unfold.
(Photo: G. Sroufe.)

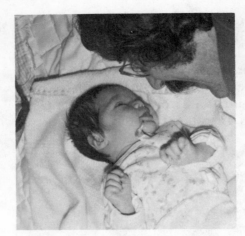

Figure 10-4.
Fathers can be
actively involved
in the infant's
care and
development
from the very
beginning.
(Photo: J. Wray.)

be involved actively with the baby, both for the sake of their attachment relationship and so that the primary caregiver not feel abandoned or feel that it is *her* baby. An active role does not necessarily mean doing the same things with the same frequency. As I hope is clear by now, important things happen outside of feeding and other physical care arenas, most especially in caregiver–infant play. Moreover, during the second year when the baby must in a way begin breaking the tie (transforming the tie) with the primary caregiver, a warm relationship with a second adult can be very important. It also may be that fathers are well able to adapt to the new pattern of toddler–caregiver interaction, since they enjoy it and may not have been involved so heavily in the early nurturance activities.

From Secure Attachment
to Emotional Involvement

In concluding this description of development, I would like to give you some idea of what you might expect this infant you have loved and enjoyed to be like as a preschool child. Though you may experience the challenge of the second-year crisis and even may experience trying times for periods all the way through the third year (until about age three or three and a half), you have every reason to expect that your delightful baby will be a delightful, bright-eyed, preschool child.

Our research has turned up what we call the "emotionally involved" preschool child. This child is eager and enthusiastic, full of life, and competent with nursery school teachers and peers. It approaches new problems and new experiences with a zestful attitude and positive expectations. It has developed skill with the inanimate world through play and exploration, and it expects positive experiences to come out of new or challenging circumstances. It moves toward life. It is not easily frustrated, does not give up readily, and is confident in its resourcefulness. When it really does get stuck, it knows how to seek and get help from adults and how to use that help effectively.

It is not surprising that such a child is well liked by the nursery school staff. Not only is it highly responsive to their efforts; it is a source of life and spirit for the entire group. It is a competent and interesting child. This child also knows how to ask for help and how to get adult attention and care through positive interactions rather than noxious, attention-seeking behavior.

Such a child also is regarded highly by peers. And why not? This is the child who knows how to exploit situations for their positive aspects. This child is where the fun is. And it is competent in dealing with objects, people, and problems. There is much to learn from such a child, and this child is also attractive because of its affective expressiveness and its empathic involvement with others. Our research has shown that children other children consistently watch are popular with teachers as well as peers, are skilled in object mastery, and are affectively expressive.

Your high-quality attachment relationship logically leads to this zestful, competent child. It is skilled in object mastery, because you have allowed and supported its exploration and mastery. It approaches problems confidently and eagerly because it has learned to believe in its resources and that adult support is there when needed. It has positive expectations concerning people and warm feelings for others because of your reliability and emotional closeness. And it is affectively expressive because it has been affectively engaged with you and because it is an alive, feeling, and happy child.

Sources

BREGER, L. *From instinct to identity: The development of personality.* Englewood Cliffs, N.J.: Prentice-Hall, Inc., 1974.

KIERKEGAARD, S. *Purity of heart is to will one thing.* New York: Harper and Row, 1938.

MAHLER, M. *The psychological birth of the infant.* New York: Basic Books, 1975.

MATAS, L. The consequences of individual differences in attachment for adaptation at age two. Unpublished doctoral dissertation, University of Minnesota, 1977.

PIAGET, J. *The origins of intelligence in children.* New York: Routledge & Kegan Paul, 1952.

SANDER, L. Issues in early mother–child interaction. *Journal of the American Academy of Child Psychiatry,* 1962, *1,* 141–66.

SROUFE, L. A. The ontogenesis of the emotions. In J. Osofsky (Ed.), *Handbook of infant development.* New York: John Wiley and Sons, Inc., in press.

SROUFE, L. A., & MITCHELL, P. Emotional development. In J. Osofsky (Ed.), *Handbook of infant development*. New York: John Wiley and Sons, Inc., in press.

SROUFE, L. A., & WATERS, E. Attachment as an organizational construct. *Child Development*, in press.

TENNES, K., EMDE, R., KISLEY, A., & METCALF, D. The stimulus barrier in early infancy. An exploration of some formulations of John Benjamin. In R. Holt & E. Peterfreund (Eds.), *Psychoanalysis and contemporary science*. New York: Macmillan, 1972.

OBSERVING
YOUR BABY

Observing
Your Baby

I am sure you will see things I never saw. . . . you are caring for, knowing, and enjoying your baby in a way that only a caregiver can.

Introduction

Throughout this book I have described the wonders of development in the first two years. Probably, without further direction from me, you would be able to see with your own eyes much of what has been discussed. Some specific suggestions for observation might be helpful, however; and there are a number of matters that you could help clarify. For example, the discussions of anger and shame have been quite speculative. I presented my best guesses, but they were based on the limited information available. You might note whether you find anger, as described below, to emerge quite suddenly or gradually and how closely it relates to persistence and other signs of "intentional" behavior. As another example, you might note the relationship between shame and self-assertion. Other questions will be presented throughout this chapter, including some that have not been answered to date.

In the following sections you will find descriptions of how to observe some of the behaviors developmental psychologists commonly study, as well as some affective and social behaviors emphasized in this book. There will be little discussion of ages and no presentation of norms (ages when most babies do something). Be especially concerned with sequences of development and the coordination of various aspects of psychological growth. I hope to discourage efforts to determine your infant's intelligence. The idea is for this guide for systematic observation of your infant to add to your interest and enjoyment of your baby and to help make some of the abstractions in this book more real.

If you would like, you may fill in the chart at the end of the chapter and send it to me. Simply record the month that you observe the appearance of the behavior in question. Make your observations only once a month on the baby's monthly birthday. In this way I can get some information on sequences of development. For example, I can find out whether the use of a support to obtain an object and the "understanding" of the use of a support (described below) commonly develop one month or two months earlier than "specific anger," or two months later, or at the same month, and so forth. Any of these are possible. Right now we really don't know. There are many important questions concerning developmental sequences and coordination that could be approached through observations of parents and others who care

for infants.

The chart only includes some of the observations I will describe, since I did not want to make
this a big job for you. Please only record observations to the extent that you enjoy doing it. Don't
do any of this if it will detract from your pleasure
in caregiving. On the other hand, you may wish to
record systematically many or all of the developments outlined below. If you do, I would especially
appreciate hearing about anomalies—that is, if you
find something does not develop in the order
described. If a number of you report the same
thing, I will know there is a need for revision
in this material. Let me repeat that I want you to
feel no obligation to make these observations or
to send them to me. The idea is that making the
observations might make the book and baby-
rearing more interesting and enjoyable. That is
the only reason for doing them.

Reflexes of Early Infancy

Though I am not suggesting that you record your
observations of early reflexes, parents frequently
find such behaviors very interesting. To see your
baby grasp and "root" will assure you of its competence, however reflexive that competence may
be. To see your newborn's crawling movements
and stepping movements will promise of things to
come. And to see the decline of many of these
reflexive behaviors over the first few months will
inform you that behavior is coming under the control of the more evolved brain mechanisms, specifically the cerebral cortex, that part of the brain
that ultimately will control memory, thought,
reasoning, and judgment.

Palmer and Planter Grasps

If you gently press your index finger in your infant's palm, your baby will grasp it forcefully, even as early as the first day of life. Similarly, if you press your thumbs gently on the balls of your baby's feet, its toes will flex as if to grasp your thumbs. The state of the infant (whether alert or sleepy) is important in making such observations. For example, infants will grasp more forcefully before or during feeding than after feeding when they are drowsy.

Babinski Reflex

Prechtl[1] suggests eliciting this reflex by scratching the outside of the sole of the foot with the thumbnail. With the baby lying on its back, feet toward you, scratch from the toes toward the heels. This will produce the characteristic spreading of the toes.

Babkin-Palmer Mental Reflex

In the early weeks and months, pressing on the infant's palms produces the reflexes of mouth-opening and eye-closing. This reflex, a number of blinking reflexes (e.g., blinking caused by tapping on the bridge of the nose), and the rooting reflex (see below) all drop out by about three months of life, the same age at which fussiness and the neonatal sleep smile drop out and when the social smile becomes reliable. All of this tells you the cerebral cortex is maturing.

---

[1] Prechtl, H., & Beintema, D. *The neurological examination of the full term newborn.* London: Heineman Medical Books, Ltd., 1964.

Rooting

This is a reflex that is obvious to caregivers in the first days of life. Touching the corner of the mouth with nipple or finger causes the infant's head to turn in that direction. Stimulation of the upper lip produces turning up of the head and opening of the mouth. Jaw-dropping and open mouth is produced by touching the lower lip.

Moro Reflex

Moro originally observed that when the surface on which the infant is lying is struck with the hands, the baby's arms spread and then come together in an arc over the body in quite a rapid and intense movement. You probably will observe this reflex in the natural course of events when there are sudden, sharp sounds near the infant or when the infant experiences a brief loss of support. One evolutionary speculation about this reflex is that it may have served to make catching onto mother or something else more likely when the newborn primate started falling.

Crawling Response

After about the third day of life, you may observe crawling movements of the legs when your infant is lying on its stomach. Such movements can be specifically produced by pressing your thumbs against the soles of your baby's feet. This is another behavior that drops out after three or four months, to appear later in the form of voluntary crawling. **179**

If you hold your infant upright, letting its feet touch a solid surface, the legs will extend and then make alternating stepping movements, especially if the trunk is bent slightly forward (Prechtl). Do not "walk" the baby, but allow it to move forward as it steps. You will see that the arms and the trunk are not involved, so these movements are different in a basic way from walking. Still, the stepping movements are rhythmic and coordinated, the reflexive version of later walking. They drop out by the fourth or fifth month.

Early Sensorimotor Accomplishments

Beyond descriptions given in Chapter 7, I would emphasize that when you note the capacity of the infant to lift its head and trunk and hold them up, for example, consider the motivational features. Why does the baby lift its head and sustain this strenuous activity? How does this development coincide with the lengthening periods of being awake and alert and the capacity to visually follow and turn to the source of sounds? Very early, babies will track a slowly moving target visually. Later they will turn to the source of a sound. Later still they will continue looking at the place where an object disappears. Where does head-lifting occur in this sequence?

The emergence of hand–eye coordination is a crucial development, important for the coordination of schemes and the beginning sense of effectance. You know that newborns will grasp objects that touch their palms. Some observers argue that very early infants will also shape their hands in rough

180

correspondence to the shape and size of objects and move their arms in the direction of objects only when they are "within reach." I also have observed a precursor of directed reaching in the early months. The infant seems to orient the entire body and being toward the object. It swings its arms in movements that do not look entirely random and actually has some success in batting objects, perhaps even in grasping. But the process of directed reaching unfolds over several months, until the infant surely, steadily, and precisely grasp any object within reach. This sequence provides an excellent opportunity for you to see both gradual, continuous development and periods of rapid change and to decide which description of this development is most fitting.

Affective Development

You already are well prepared to observe many important aspects of the development of affect and affective expression. Along with motor achievements, these are the most visible manifestations of development, and they are absolutely central for forming a picture of the changing mental life of the child. Affect not only *is influenced by* cognitive development; it *reflects changes* in cognitive development as well. Just knowing the importance of affect will guide you a great deal in observing your baby. Some guidelines for specific things to observe are presented below.

Newborn Smiles

Newborn sleep smiles are described in Chapter 3. You are most likely to see these when your baby is just falling off to sleep (perhaps after feeding) or just waking. Recall that they occur during REM sleep, so a fluttering of the eyelids will signal you that such smiles are likely. You also may have success in producing these smiles by gently rousing the baby to the threshold of wakefulness. Soon you also can produce them with a rattle, chime, or other gentle, repetitive stimulation. Remember, in early weeks there will be a notable delay between the stimulation and the smile. Don't be disappointed if you cannot get these all the time or even if you have trouble getting them at all. You *will* see the sleep smiles, and you will see the alert and awake smiles to more vigorous stimulation later. And you will see the smile to your face. See how closely your observations agree with the discussion in Chapter 3 and the sequence outlined in Table 3-1.

*The Progression of Smiling
and Laughter*

The progression of smiling and laughter is outlined in Chapters 3 and 4. Try all of our procedures for eliciting laughter (Table 4-2). Do these just once a month. Try each item up to six times. Make sure you pause between each presentation and especially between items. Obviously, if the baby is laughing at one item it may spill over to others, and you would not know whether the reaction was really to the new item. When we make these observations we also present the items in a different order each month to further rule out systematic contagion effects. We usually took two days to do all of the items, since when babies get fatigued they will not laugh.

Does laughter to the items follow the sequence outlined in Chapter 4? If an item upsets the baby at four months, is it likely to produce laughter the following month? Does laughter routinely build from smiling, or does the baby sometimes cry on the first presentation, then laugh?

Also notice some of the changes in the quality of laughter behavior. When does the baby begin trying to get you to repeat the games, for example, leaning its cheek toward you in "coochy-coo" or trying to put the cloth back in your mouth? When does the baby laugh in anticipation, for example, before you return in peekaboo? At this time, does it also try to pull the cover from your face? When does it initiate the games with you, in addition to merely repeating things you start? Some form of peekaboo is often the first example, with the child popping in and out of a doorway or hiding something, then reproducing it. When do you see "original games" created by the child to its own great amusement (see Figure 4-2)? For example, I watched an infant, about age fourteen months, do a game for several minutes in a hospital lobby. She sat on the edge of a couch with her feet dangling. Then, smiling, she slid forward until her feet hit the floor and she tumbled forward. Grinning from ear to ear, she climbed up to repeat the game several times. She would look at the spectators, grin, then tumble off. She was completely delighted and completely delightful. She created this game, initiated it, timed it, and paused for effect.

I would like to have more information concerning these questions. I am also confident that you will find these observations enjoyable, because I know hundreds of parents who have carried out these procedures.

Anger, Fear, and Shame

I do not suggest that you do anything to frighten or make your baby angry. Don't worry, these reactions will occur in the natural course of events. **183**

How early distress and rage evolve to fear and anger has been described. I am especially interested in the relationship between these reactions and cognitive development (below). Especially pay attention to the development of specific anger and clear-cut fear. When, for example, does the infant show an immediate angry response when an action is blocked (that is, rather than distress building up, the infant shifts from a positive tone or mood to intense motor behavior [flailing] or crying quite rapidly)? It may be trying to get an object or do something it cannot. Suddenly, in face and behavior it shows you it is angry (see Figure 11-1b). Similarly, when does it turn from, retreat from, or cry quite quickly when a stranger tries to pick it up or even just approach it? At what age does it cry at the sight of the doctor? Is it more negative to unknown persons after trips to the doctor? When do you first see fear faces (Figure 11-1c)? These may not appear until the second year, although you may see subtle signs of negative reactions much earlier.

When do you see the facial expression of shame (Figure 11-1d)? These probably will follow sensitivity to scolding by some months. Parents often report "sheepish" expressions much earlier than I believe true shame to develop.

Affection

When with respect to anger, fear, and shame do you find signs of affection developing? When, for example, does your infant give you "love pats"? When does it hug its dolls or comfort another baby or child? How do these developments relate to mirror recognition?

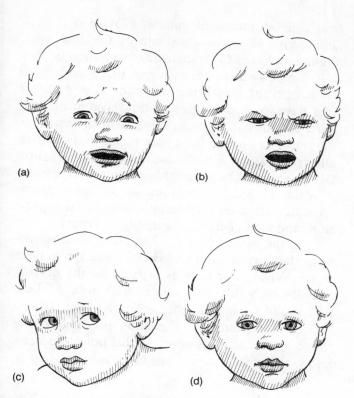

Figure 11-1 a-d: The faces of fear (a), anger (b), and shame (c), compared with an affectively neutral, attentive expression (d). (Illustration: J. Roberts.)

Mirror Observations

In our studies we observed that babies begin smiling at their image in the mirror not long after they began smiling regularly at faces. In the months that followed some even laughed. Vigorous smiling and laughter peaked at seven months. They did not lose interest after this point; on the contrary, they were quite attentive (Figure 11-1a). We thought there **185**

was a development of curious ("Who is that?")
and even coy expressions late in the first year,
though we have little systematic information on this.

To make these observations, place the baby in
front of a full-length mirror or the largest mirror
you have. You will have to hold young infants;
older infants can be in an infant seat or seated on
the floor. Try not to have your image in the mirror
and try to avoid a peekaboo or gamelike quality.
Observe your baby's attentive behavior. Note when
it begins noticing its movements (or even experi-
menting with these). Especially note facial expressions and affect (smiling, laughing, curiosity).

In the second year you can make the observations that Amsterdam and Brooks and Lewis have
made. When your baby is in front of the mirror,
unobtrusively rub some rouge on its nose. Make a
pretense of wiping the nose with a Kleenex. Check
for the appearance of the baby reacting to the
rouge by touching its nose. At this point the baby
knows that it is *its own* image in the mirror.

Cognitive Development

Exploring the Environment

Mouthing and visual inspection are early exploratory
behaviors of the infant. Later these will be com-
bined with reaching, and for a time every object
the infant sees within reach will be grasped and
brought to mouth. (I have seen them even attempt
a beach ball!)

The following is a developmental sequence
you can watch unfold. Quite early the infant will
hit and pat objects with the hand or will knock
two objects together. Slightly later it will shake or

wave objects, apparently to note the effects of these actions. Quite a bit later, it will drop objects and watch them fall. Throwing objects develops later. Making objects perform task-appropriate actions (e.g., "driving" a car) is an even later development. Finally showing and naming objects will emerge.

Visual Pursuit and the Permanence of Objects

Learning that objects exist and continue to exist even when in different perspective or when they're not even present is a major cognitive achievement in infancy. The following is a widely accepted sequence in the unfolding of this capacity.

At first your infant will follow a slowly moving object with its eyes as you move it in a complete 180-degree arc from one side of its face to the other. (Hold the object about 18 inches away from the infant's face and repeat this several times.) Young infants will stop looking when the object disappears. Later, their glance will linger at the spot where the object vanished from sight. Following several presentations, they may even return their eyes to the place of origin in anticipation of the next presentation. At a later point, the infant will retrieve an object that you only partially cover with a cloth. Finally, it will uncover and retrieve an object that you covered completely. In a sense, it now knows that objects exist even when it cannot see them. All of this happens in the first year.

In the second year the infant develops the knowledge that objects act or change independent of its actions. For example, first hide the object under one cloth and let the baby get it. Then, hide the object in three successive places, not letting the infant see the object hidden in your hand, but letting it see your hand move from hiding place to hiding place. At what age does it go immediately to the third hiding place, rather than to the place where it previously found the object?

Development of Means for Obtaining Objects or Consequences

Another important cognitive ability concerns what can be called means–ends relationships. Very early, shaking a rattle produces noise. Much later a toy can be reached with a stick as an early exercise of tool-using capacity.

The beginning of this cognitive capacity is visually guided reaching. The hand is the first tool for acting on objects. Shaking rattles or knocking musical toys comes next (though as early as eight weeks infants can learn to kick their feet to make a mobile turn). Next, the infant learns that it must let go of one block to grasp another when both hands are full. (Simply hand the baby one block, then another; and while it is holding one in each hand, offer it a third. At first it will try for all three with predictable consequences.) Moving its own body to retrieve an object comes later. Even later the infant begins getting the idea of the use of a support. Place a toy on a pillow or cloth, with the toy at the opposite end but the pillow in easy reach. Does it pull the support to get the object? Or will it do this after you demonstrate the use of the support? At what age? To see if it "understands" the relationship of support, next hold the toy above the support. While this is a difficult test to do, the idea is that the baby will not pull the support unless the object is on it. This will be a later development than simply using the support with or without demonstration.

At the end of the first year or in the second year you also may try the following procedures. (1) Tie a string around an object, and set the object across the table from the baby. Leave the end of the string readily within reach. See if the baby gets the object without a demonstration. If not, demonstrate for it. This is *relatively* easy, since the baby can pull on the string in a haphazard fashion and can let go of the string before picking up the object. Much more difficult is the vertical use of the string. (2) Here the object the baby sees and wants is on the floor tied to the string that you give the baby. At earlier ages it may simply play with the string or drop the string on the floor. But now it may try to pull up the desired object. Note that this requires very difficult hand-over-hand movements and that if the baby lets go of the string before grasping the object it cannot get it. (3) You also can see when the baby can use a stick to get an object that is out of reach, with and without a demonstration by you. Always let the baby work on the problem first, before demonstrating.

The Development
of Operational Causality

Operational causality is related to means–ends. Here, however, the emphasis is on the infant learning that *it* is a cause of events, rather than learning that there are causes of events and means for producing causes. Again, there is an agreed-upon developmental sequence underlying this sense of causation. You may be impressed by the importance of affect in the examples below.

An early sign of the dawning of a sense of causation is the baby showing some behavior indicating its wish for you to repeat a game or spectacle. For example, when you bounce it on your knees, then pause, it may kick its feet or bounce as a sign that it wants more. Or it may attempt to move your arm to get you to carry out an action again. Later, this behavior becomes more specific. It may hand you back the cloth for peekaboo, attempt to put the cloth back in your mouth in our laughter item, hand you the string for the "jumping jack." Finally it will be able to initiate games with you or reactivate a mechanical toy by itself. Throughout this sequence there is a progressive involvement of the infant, from merely signaling its desire for the spectacle to be repeated, to helping you to repeat it, to bringing it about by itself.

Behavioral Organization

Though there is much to see, there is little that would be easy to chart in terms of the organization of behavior and the interaction of behavioral systems. You will observe things developing at the same time, and you will observe developmental sequences. Somewhat more subtle is the interaction among behavioral systems.

Try to notice especially the interaction of attachment, exploration, wariness, and affiliation by the end of the first year of life. Does the baby stay by you at first, then move out to explore when you are together in a new setting? Does it range away from you, occasionally checking back and setting off again? Does it for a time visually check out new people from your side (and your reactions to them), then warm up and become engaged with them? When hurt or frightened, does it seek you

Observational Chart

In filling out the developmental chart (Table 11-1), simply record the month you first observe each behavior. In the case of naturally occurring behaviors, record them on the following monthly birthday. For example, when your baby is exactly eight months old, you do the mirror observations, covered-object test, laughter items, and so forth. If the baby first shows the behavior in question at this testing, you record an 8 next to that item. You also record an 8 next to any behavior (e.g., specific anger) you saw occur during the month since your monthly observation at seven months.

You probably will learn quickly that you do not have to do all the items each month. Some obviously will be way beyond your baby's capacity at a particular age. Virtually none of these will appear in the first half-year (perhaps only "lingering glance"). Also, once the baby shows a behavior clearly, you do not have to repeat it the next month, although this is a good idea. Sometimes you will see how much more solid a capacity becomes after it emerges.

All of the items except for the imitation, persistence, showing, and pretending items are described in this chapter or the smiling and laughter chapters. Page numbers are given in the chart so that you can find these descriptions easily.

On the back of the chart there is a space for describing games your baby creates. I am very interested in cataloguing these games infants originate. There is also a space to list anomalies, aspects of behavior, or sequences of behavior you **191** observe that are not in agreement with descriptions in this book. If you wish to send the chart to me, my address is Institute of Child Development, 51 East River Road, University of Minnesota, Minneapolis, Minnesota, 55455.

Conclusion

The heaviest emphasis in this chapter has been on observations to make in the second six months, with little stress on development in the second year. Except for one imitation item, for example, no observations on the development of language are suggested; yet language is a crucial and fascinating area of development. Like everything else we have discussed, language acquisition illustrates the organized view of development. Early language apparently is influenced by emotional development and affect, and it clearly contributes to social and emotional development as well. Self-assertion ("Me," "I," "No," and "Do it myself") is clearly an impetus for language, as well as being reflected in language.

Still, I have provided no guidelines for such observations. But by now you can do it. You understand the developmental approach to infant and toddler behavior. You tell me of your interesting or exciting observations in the second year. How does language relate to shame and affection? How does it relate to the continuing development of memory and knowledge about objects? I also would like to hear of intriguing things you discover that are not even mentioned in this book. I am sure you will see things I never saw. After all, you are caring for, knowing, and enjoying your baby in a way that only a caregiver can.

Table 11-1:   Developmental Chart

Affective and Social Development	Month Appeared	Cognitive Development	Month Appeared
Mirror Behavior (p. 185)		Exploration (p. 186)	
—sober attention to mirror	_____	—dropping objects, watching fall	_____
—"coy" expressions to mirror	_____	Object Concept (p. 188)	
—mirror recognition	_____	—lingering glance	_____
Laughter (Chapter 4)		—retrieves partially covered	_____
—anticipatory laughter	_____	—retrieves fully covered	_____
—laughter to cloth-in-mouth	_____	—finds with three hidings	_____
—laughter to mother sucking bottle	_____	Means–Ends (p. 189)	
Fear and Anger (p. 184)		—using a support	_____
—avoidance of strangers	_____	—"understanding" support	_____
—crying to strangers	_____	—vertical string	_____
—conditioned fear (crying on sight of doctor or other)	_____	—use of stick	_____
		Operational Causality (p. 189)	
—separation protest (regularly crying when you leave the room)	_____	—signals desire for repetition	_____
		—participates in game (pulls cloth off)	_____
—specific anger	_____	—acts to get you to repeat game	
Shame (p. 183)		(puts cloth back in your mouth)	_____
—reaction to scolding	_____	—initiates the game	_____
—shame face	_____	—self games*	_____
Affection (p. 184)		Imitation	
—hugging dolls	_____	—imitates familiar words	_____
—comforting others	_____	—imitates novel gestures:touch your ear, pat top of your head	
—love pats	_____		_____
Showing and Pretending		Persistence	
—regularly shows toys to you	_____	—pursues an object it cannot get	_____
—pretends to drink from cup	_____	—will not be distracted from object	_____

*On the reverse of this page describe this game. I am interested in cataloguing games infants invent.

Table 11-1

Description of Novel Games

*Anomalies (Observations you made that do not agree with sequences
or behaviors described in this book.)*

Index